tapas
100 everyday recipes

First published in 2011
LOVE FOOD is an imprint of Parragon Books Ltd

Parragon
Chartist House
15-17 Trim Street
Bath BA1 1HA, UK
www.parragon.com

ISBN: 978-1-4454-4289-1

Printed in China

Produced by Ivy Contract
Cover photography by Mike Cooper
Cover image home economy and food styling by Lincoln Jefferson

Notes for the Reader

This book uses imperial, metric, and US cup measurements. Follow the same units of measurement throughout; do not mix imperial and metric. All spoon measurements are level: teaspoons are assumed to be 5 ml, and tablespoons are assumed to be 15 ml. Unless otherwise stated, milk is assumed to be whole, eggs and individual vegetables, such as potatoes, are medium, and pepper is freshly ground black pepper.

The times given are an approximate guide only. Preparation times differ according to the techniques used by different people and the cooking times may also vary from those given as a result of the type of oven used. Optional ingredients, variations, or serving suggestions have not been included in the calculations.

Recipes using raw or very lightly cooked eggs should be avoided by infants, the elderly, pregnant women, convalescents, and anyone with a chronic condition. Pregnant and breast-feeding women are advised to avoid eating peanuts and peanut products. People with nut allergies should be aware that some of the prepared ingredients used in the recipes in this book may contain nuts. Always check the package before use.

tapas

introduction

Tapas has become a bit of a buzzword in the last few years, but what exactly is tapas, and where does it come from?

Tapas is the collective name for small, delicious mouthfuls of something savory, served with a chilled white wine, beer, or sherry. It comes from tapa, the Spanish word for lid—specifically, the "lid" created by the slice of bread that an innkeeper would thoughtfully place on top of a customer's wine glass to keep out the flies and dust between sips. The Andalucians then came up with the idea of balancing a morsel of something tasty on top of the bread to nibble on—a few slices of cheese or ham—and a new Spanish institution was born. Today, tapas are served in almost every bar throughout Spain. Usually they are displayed on the bar, and the waiter puts your selection on a plate, for eating either standing up or seated at the bar or a table.

Everything about tapas, from the preparation to eating and enjoying it, is a uniquely Spanish experience. Tapas are what eating is all about, a true feast for the senses—they look and smell delectable, and taste even better. Serve them on pretty plates in bright colors to bring a little Spanish sunshine to a cloudy day.

How you use tapas is up to you. A simple selection of these bite-size gastronomic glories can be served with drinks before lunch or dinner, or an array of dishes can make an informal lunch or dinner in themselves. Tapas are made from a wonderful variety of foods—meat, seafood, eggs, nuts, and cheese, as well as every vibrant vegetable imaginable, in healthy Mediterranean style, with dips and sauces to add even more flavor and interest to the tapas experience.

Eating tapas goes hand-in-hand with hospitality, friendship, and plenty of good conversation, so tuck in, forget the cares of the day, and linger, Spanish-style, with your favorite people.

nibbles

deep-fried green chiles

ingredients

serves 4–6

olive oil, for frying
9 oz/250 g sweet or hot
    fresh chiles
sea salt

method

1 Heat 3 inches/7.5 cm of oil in a large, heavy-bottom pan until it reaches 350–375°F/180–190°C, or until a cube of bread turns brown in 30 seconds.

2 Rinse the chiles and pat them very dry with paper towels. Drop them in the hot oil for no longer than 20 seconds, or until they turn bright green and the skins blister.

3 Remove with a slotted spoon and drain well on crumpled paper towels. Sprinkle with sea salt and serve immediately.

tomato bread

ingredients

serves 4

4 slices French bread
2 ripe tomatoes, halved
1 garlic clove, finely chopped
    (optional)
2 tbsp olive oil (optional)

method

1 Preheat the broiler. Toast the bread until lightly golden on both sides.

2 Rub each slice of bread with half a fresh juicy tomato. If using, sprinkle over the chopped garlic and drizzle the olive oil over the top.

spareribs coated in paprika sauce

ingredients

serves 6

olive oil, for oiling
2 lb 12 oz/1.25 kg pork
    spareribs
⅓ cup dry Spanish sherry
5 tsp hot or sweet smoked
    Spanish paprika
2 garlic cloves, crushed
1 tbsp dried oregano
⅔ cup water
salt

method

1 Oil a large roasting pan. If the butcher has not already done so, cut the sheets of spareribs into individual ribs. If possible, cut each sparerib in half widthwise. Put the spareribs in the prepared pan, in a single layer, and roast in a preheated oven, 425°F/220°C, for 20 minutes.

2 Meanwhile, make the sauce. Put the sherry, paprika, garlic, oregano, water, and salt to taste in a pitcher and mix together well.

3 Reduce the oven temperature to 350°F/180°C. Pour off the fat from the pan, then pour the sauce over the spareribs and turn the spareribs to coat with the sauce on both sides. Roast for an additional 45 minutes, basting the spareribs with the sauce once halfway through the cooking time, until tender.

4 Pile the spareribs into a warmed serving dish. Bring the sauce in the roasting pan to a boil on the stove, then reduce the heat and simmer until reduced by half. Pour the sauce over the spareribs and serve hot.

pan-fried shrimp

ingredients

serves 4

4 garlic cloves
20–24 large shrimp, peeled
generous ½ cup butter
¼ cup olive oil
⅓ cup brandy
salt and pepper
2 tbsp chopped fresh parsley,
    to garnish
lemon wedges, to serve

method

1 Using a sharp knife, peel and slice the garlic.

2 Wash the shrimp and pat dry using paper towels.

3 Melt the butter with the oil in a large skillet, add the garlic and shrimp, and fry over high heat, stirring, for 3–4 minutes, until the shrimp are pink.

4 Sprinkle with brandy and season with salt and pepper to taste. Sprinkle with parsley and serve immediately with lemon wedges, for squeezing over the shrimp.

variation

Instead of the brandy, use 1 tablespoon of soy sauce, 1 tablespoon of rice wine, and a teaspoon of sugar.

sun-dried tomato & goat cheese tarts

ingredients

serves 6

2¹/₂ oz/70 g sun-dried tomatoes in oil, drained and 2 tbsp oil reserved

1 zucchini, thinly sliced

1 garlic clove, crushed

9 oz/250 g puff pastry, thawed if frozen

5¹/₂ oz/150 g soft goat cheese

salt and pepper

method

1 Dampen a large cookie sheet. Finely chop the sun-dried tomatoes and reserve. Heat 1 tablespoon of the reserved oil from the tomatoes in a large skillet, then add the zucchini slices and cook over medium heat, stirring occasionally, for 8–10 minutes, or until golden brown on both sides. Add the garlic and cook, stirring, for 30 seconds. Remove from the heat and let cool while you prepare the pastry bases.

2 Thinly roll out the pastry on a lightly floured counter. Using a plain, 3¹/₂-inch/9-cm cutter, cut out 1–2 circles, rerolling the trimmings as necessary. Transfer the circles to the prepared cookie sheet and prick 3–4 times with the tines of a fork. Divide the zucchini mixture equally between the pastry circles, add the tomatoes, leaving a ¹/₂-inch/1-cm border around the edge, and top each tart with a spoonful of goat cheese. Drizzle over 1 tablespoon of the remaining oil from the tomatoes and season to taste with salt and pepper.

3 Bake the tarts in a preheated oven, 425°F/220°C, for 10–15 minutes, or until golden brown and well risen. Serve warm.

moroccan chicken kabobs

ingredients

serves 4

1 lb/450 g chicken breast fillets
3 tbsp olive oil, plus extra for oiling
juice of 1 lemon
2 garlic cloves, crushed
1½ tsp ground cumin
1 tsp ground coriander
1 tsp hot or sweet smoked
     Spanish paprika
¼ tsp ground cinnamon
½ tsp dried oregano
salt
chopped fresh flat-leaf parsley,
     to garnish

method

1 Cut the chicken into 1-inch/2.5-cm cubes and put in a large, shallow, nonmetallic dish. Put all the remaining ingredients, except the parsley, in a bowl and whisk together. Pour the marinade over the chicken cubes and toss the meat in the marinade until well coated. Cover and let marinate in the refrigerator for 8 hours or overnight, turning the chicken 2–3 times if possible.

2 If using wooden skewers or toothpicks, soak the skewers in cold water for about 30 minutes to help prevent them from burning and the food sticking to them during cooking. If using metal skewers, lightly brush with oil. Preheat the broiler or grill pan. Remove the chicken pieces from the marinade, reserving the remaining marinade, and thread an equal quantity onto each prepared skewer or toothpick, leaving a little space between each piece.

3 Brush the broiler rack or grill pan with a little oil. Preheat the broiler and add the kabobs and cook, turning frequently and brushing with the reserved marinade halfway through cooking, for 15 minutes, or until browned on all sides, tender, and cooked through. Serve hot, sprinkled with chopped parsley to garnish.

zucchini fritters

ingredients

serves 6–8

1 lb/450 g baby zucchini
3 tbsp all-purpose flour
1 tsp paprika
1 large egg
2 tbsp milk
corn oil, for pan-frying
coarse sea salt

pine nut sauce
²/₃ cup pine nuts
1 garlic clove, peeled
3 tbsp extra virgin olive oil
1 tbsp lemon juice
3 tbsp water
1 tbsp chopped fresh
    flat-leaf parsley
salt and pepper

method

1 To make the pine nut sauce, place the pine nuts and garlic in a food processor and process to form a paste. With the motor still running, gradually add the olive oil, lemon juice, and water to form a smooth sauce. Stir in the parsley and season to taste with salt and pepper. Transfer to a serving bowl and reserve until needed.

2 To prepare the zucchini, cut them on the diagonal into thin slices about ¼ inch/5 mm thick. Place the flour and paprika in a plastic bag and mix together. Beat the egg and milk together in a large bowl.

3 Add the zucchini slices to the flour mixture and toss well together until coated. Shake off the excess flour. Heat the corn oil in a large, heavy-bottom skillet to a depth of about ½ inch/1 cm. Dip the zucchini slices, one at a time, into the egg mixture, then slip them into the hot oil. Cook the zucchini slices in batches in a single layer so that they do not overcrowd the skillet, for 2 minutes, or until they are crisp and golden brown.

4 Using a slotted spoon, remove the zucchini fritters from the skillet and drain on paper towels. Continue until all the zucchini slices have been fried.

5 Serve the zucchini fritters piping hot, lightly sprinkled with sea salt, and accompanied by the pine nut sauce for dipping.

olives with orange & lemon

ingredients

serves 4–6

2 tsp fennel seeds
2 tsp cumin seeds
1¼ cups green olives
1¼ cups black olives
2 tsp grated orange rind
2 tsp grated lemon rind
3 shallots, finely chopped
pinch of ground cinnamon
¼ cup white wine vinegar
scant ⅓ cup olive oil
2 tbsp orange juice
1 tbsp chopped fresh mint
1 tbsp chopped fresh parsley

method

1 Dry-fry the fennel seeds and cumin seeds in a small, heavy-bottom skillet, shaking the skillet frequently, until they begin to pop and give off their aroma. Remove the skillet from the heat and let cool.

2 Place the olives, orange and lemon rind, shallots, cinnamon, and toasted seeds in a bowl.

3 Whisk the vinegar, olive oil, orange juice, mint, and parsley together in a bowl and pour over the olives. Toss well, then cover and let chill in the refrigerator for 1–2 days before serving.

cracked marinated olives

ingredients

serves 8

1 lb/450 g can or jar unpitted
     large green olives, drained
4 garlic cloves, peeled
2 tsp coriander seeds
1 small lemon
4 sprigs of fresh thyme
4 feathery stalks of fennel
2 small fresh red chiles (optional)
pepper
extra virgin olive oil, to cover

method

1 To allow the flavors of the marinade to penetrate the olives, place the olives on a cutting board and, using a rolling pin, bash them lightly so that they crack slightly. Alternatively, use a sharp knife to cut a lengthwise slit in each olive as far as the pit. Using the flat side of a broad knife, lightly crush each garlic clove. Using a mortar and pestle, crack the coriander seeds. Cut the lemon, with its rind, into small chunks.

2 Put the olives, garlic, coriander seeds, lemon chunks, thyme sprigs, fennel, and chiles, if using, in a large bowl and toss together. Season with pepper to taste, but you should not need to add salt as preserved olives are usually salty enough. Pack the ingredients tightly into a glass jar with a lid. Pour in enough olive oil to cover the olives, then seal the jar tightly.

3 Let the olives stand at room temperature for 24 hours, then marinate in the refrigerator for at least one week but preferably two weeks before serving. From time to time, gently give the jar a shake to remix the ingredients. Return the olives to room temperature and remove from the oil to serve. Provide toothpicks for spearing the olives.

paprika-spiced almonds

ingredients

serves 4–6

1½ tbsp coarse sea salt
½ tsp smoked sweet Spanish
    paprika, or hot paprika, to taste
generous 2 cups blanched almonds
extra virgin olive oil

method

1 Place the sea salt and paprika in a mortar and grind with the pestle to a fine powder. Alternatively, use a mini spice blender (the amount is too small to process in a full-size processor).

2 Place the almonds on a cookie sheet and toast in a preheated oven, 400°F/200°C, for 8–10 minutes, stirring occasionally, until golden and giving off a toasted aroma. Watch after 7 minutes because they burn quickly. Pour into a heatproof bowl.

3 Drizzle over 1 tablespoon of olive oil and stir to ensure all the nuts are lightly and evenly coated. Add extra oil if necessary. Sprinkle with the salt and paprika mixture and stir again. Transfer to a small bowl and serve at room temperature.

variation

For a sweeter flavour, mix together ¼ cup of sugar, 1 teaspoon of cinnamon, ½ teaspoon of cumin, and less paprika to taste.

salted almonds

ingredients

serves 4–6

scant 1½ cups whole almonds,
   in their skins or blanched
   (see method)
¼ cup olive oil
coarse sea salt
1 tsp paprika or ground cumin
   (optional)

method

1 Fresh almonds in their skins are superior in taste, but
   blanched almonds are much more convenient. If the
   almonds are not blanched, put them in a bowl, cover
   with boiling water for 3–4 minutes, then plunge them
   into cold water for 1 minute. Drain them well in a
   strainer, then slide off the skins between your fingers.
   Dry the almonds well on paper towels.

2 Put the olive oil in a roasting pan and swirl it round so
   that it covers the bottom. Add the almonds and toss
   them in the pan so that they are evenly coated in the
   oil, then spread them out in a single layer.

3 Roast the almonds in a preheated oven, 350°F/180°C,
   for 20 minutes, or until they are light golden brown,
   tossing several times during the cooking. Drain the
   almonds on paper towels, then transfer them to a
   serving bowl.

4 While the almonds are still warm, sprinkle with plenty
   of sea salt and the paprika or cumin, if using, and toss
   well together to coat. Serve the almonds warm or cold.

   Note: The almonds are at their best when served
   freshly cooked, so, if possible, cook them on the day
   that you plan to eat them. However, they can be
   stored in an airtight container for up to three days.

eggplant & bell pepper dip

ingredients

serves 6–8

2 large eggplants
2 red bell peppers
¼ cup olive oil
2 garlic cloves, coarsely
    chopped
grated rind and juice of ½ lemon
1 tbsp chopped cilantro,
    plus extra sprigs to garnish
½–1 tsp paprika
salt and pepper
bread or toast, to serve

method

1 Prick the skins of the eggplants and bell peppers all over with a fork and brush with 1 tablespoon of the olive oil. Place on a cookie sheet and bake in a preheated oven, 375°F/190°C, for 45 minutes, or until the skins are beginning to turn black, the flesh of the eggplant is very soft, and the bell peppers are deflated.

2 Place the cooked vegetables in a bowl and cover tightly with a clean, damp dish towel. Let stand for about 15 minutes, or until cool enough to handle, then cut the eggplants in half lengthwise, carefully scoop out the flesh and discard the skin. Cut the eggplant flesh into large chunks. Remove and discard the stem, core, and seeds from the bell peppers and cut the flesh into large pieces.

3 Heat the remaining olive oil in a skillet. Add the vegetables and cook for 5 minutes. Add the garlic and cook for 30 seconds.

4 Drain the contents of the skillet on paper towels, then transfer to a food processor. Add the lemon rind and juice, the chopped cilantro, the paprika, and salt and pepper to taste, then process until a speckled purée is formed. Transfer the dip to a serving bowl. Serve warm or at room temperature. Garnish with cilantro sprigs and accompany with bread or toast.

eggplant dip

ingredients

serves 6–8

¹⁄₃ cup olive oil
1 large eggplant, about
    14 oz/400 g, sliced
2 scallions, finely chopped
1 large garlic clove, crushed
2 tbsp finely chopped
    fresh parsley
salt and pepper
smoked sweet Spanish paprika,
    to garnish
crusty bread, to serve

method

1 Heat 4 tablespoons of the olive oil in a large skillet over medium–high heat. Add the eggplant slices and cook on both sides until soft and beginning to brown. Remove from the skillet and let cool. The slices will release the oil again as they cool.

2 Heat the remaining olive oil in the skillet. Add the scallions and garlic and cook for 3 minutes, or until the scallions become soft. Remove from the heat and reserve with the eggplant slices to cool.

3 Transfer all these ingredients to a food processor and process just until a coarse purée forms. Transfer to a serving bowl and stir in the parsley. Taste and adjust the seasoning, if necessary. Serve immediately, or cover and let chill in the refrigerator until 15 minutes before required. Sprinkle with paprika and serve with crusty bread.

potato wedges with roasted garlic dip

ingredients

serves 8

3 lb/1.3 kg potatoes, unpeeled
and halved
2 tbsp olive oil
1 garlic clove, finely chopped
2 tsp salt

roasted garlic dip

2 garlic bulbs, separated
into cloves
1 tbsp olive oil
scant 1/3 cup sour cream or
strained plain yogurt
1/4 cup mayonnaise
salt
paprika, to taste

method

1 To make the roasted garlic dip, place the garlic cloves
in an ovenproof dish, pour in the olive oil and toss
to coat. Spread out in a single layer and roast in a
preheated oven, 400°F/200°C, for 25 minutes, or until
tender. Remove from the oven and let stand until cool
enough to handle.

2 Peel the garlic cloves, then place on a heavy cutting
board and sprinkle with a little salt. Mash well with a
fork until smooth. Scrape into a bowl and stir in the
sour cream and mayonnaise. Season to taste with salt
and paprika. Cover the bowl with plastic wrap and let
chill in the refrigerator until ready to serve.

3 To cook the potatoes, cut each potato half into
3 wedges and place in a large bowl. Add the olive oil,
garlic, and salt and toss well. Transfer the wedges to a
roasting pan, then arrange in a single layer and roast
in the preheated oven for 1–1 1/4 hours, or until crisp
and golden.

4 Remove the potatoes from the oven and transfer to
serving bowls. Serve immediately, handing round the
roasted garlic dip separately.

roasted asparagus with serrano ham

ingredients

serves 6

2 tbsp olive oil
6 slices Serrano ham
12 asparagus spears
pepper

aïoli

1 large egg yolk, at room
    temperature
1 tbsp white wine vinegar
    or lemon juice
2 large garlic cloves, peeled
scant $^1/_3$ cup extra virgin olive oil
scant $^1/_3$ cup corn oil
salt and pepper

method

1 To make the aïoli, blend the egg yolk, vinegar, garlic, and salt and pepper in a food processor. With the motor still running, very slowly add the olive oil, then the corn oil, drop by drop at first, then, when it starts to thicken, in a slow steady stream until the sauce is thick and smooth. Alternatively, mix in a bowl with a whisk.

2 Place half the olive oil in a roasting pan that will hold the asparagus spears in a single layer and swirl it around so that it covers the base. Cut each slice of Serrano ham in half lengthwise.

3 Trim and discard the coarse woody ends of the asparagus spears, then wrap a slice of ham around the stem end of each spear. Place the wrapped spears in the prepared roasting pan and lightly brush with the remaining olive oil. Season the asparagus with pepper.

4 Roast the asparagus spears in a preheated oven, 400°F/200°C, for 10 minutes, depending on the thickness of the asparagus, until tender but still firm. Do not overcook the asparagus spears, as it is important that they are still firm, so that you can pick them up with your fingers. Serve the roasted asparagus piping hot, accompanied by a bowl of aïoli for dipping.

chicken wings with tomato dressing

ingredients

serves 6

¾ cup olive oil

3 garlic cloves, finely chopped

1 tsp ground cumin

2 lb 4 oz/1 kg chicken wings

2 tomatoes, peeled, seeded, and diced

scant ⅓ cup white wine vinegar

1 tbsp shredded fresh basil leaves

method

1 Mix 1 tablespoon of the oil, the garlic, and cumin together in a shallow dish. Cut off and discard the tips of the chicken wings and add the wings to the spice mixture, turning to coat. Cover with plastic wrap and leave to marinate in a cool place for 15 minutes.

2 Heat 3 tablespoons of the remaining oil in a large, heavy-bottom skillet. Add the chicken wings, in batches, and cook, turning frequently, until golden brown. Transfer to a roasting pan. Roast the chicken wings in a preheated oven, 350°F/180°C, for 10–15 minutes, or until tender and the juices run clear when the point of a sharp knife is inserted into the thickest part of the meat.

3 Meanwhile, mix the remaining olive oil, the tomatoes, vinegar, and basil together in a bowl.

4 Using tongs, transfer the chicken wings to a non-metallic dish. Pour the dressing over them, turning to coat. Cover with plastic wrap, leave to cool, then let chill in the refrigerator for 4 hours. Remove from the refrigerator 30–60 minutes before serving to return the chicken wings to room temperature.

garlic pan-fried bread & chorizo

ingredients

serves 6–8

7 oz/200 g chorizo sausage,
    outer casing removed
4 thick slices 2-day-old
    country bread
olive oil, for pan-frying
3 garlic cloves, finely chopped
2 tbsp chopped fresh
    flat-leaf parsley
paprika, to garnish

method

1 Cut the chorizo sausage into ½-inch/1-cm thick slices
and cut the bread, with its crusts still on, into ½-inch/
1-cm cubes. Add enough olive oil to a large, heavy-
bottom skillet so that it generously covers the bottom.
Heat the oil, add the garlic, and cook for 30 seconds–
1 minute, or until lightly browned.

2 Add the bread cubes to the skillet and pan-fry, stirring
all the time, until golden brown and crisp. Add the
chorizo slices and pan-fry for 1–2 minutes, or until hot.
Using a slotted spoon, remove the bread cubes and
chorizo from the skillet and drain well on paper towels.

3 Turn the pan-fried bread and chorizo into a warmed
serving bowl, add the chopped parsley, and toss
together. Garnish the dish with a sprinkling of paprika
and serve warm. Accompany with toothpicks so that
a piece of sausage and a cube of bread can be speared
together for eating.

sizzling chile shrimp

ingredients

serves 8

1 lb 2 oz/500 g raw jumbo shrimp, in their shells
1 small fresh red chile
⅓ cup olive oil
2 garlic cloves, finely chopped
pinch of paprika
salt
crusty bread, to serve

method

1 To prepare the shrimp, pull off their heads. With your fingers, peel off their shells, leaving the tails intact. Using a sharp knife, make a shallow slit along the back of each shrimp, then pull out the dark vein and discard. Rinse the shrimp under cold water and dry well on paper towels.

2 Cut the chile in half lengthwise, remove the seeds, and finely chop the flesh. It is important either to wear gloves or to wash your hands very thoroughly after chopping chilies because their juices can cause irritation to sensitive skin, especially round the eyes, nose, or mouth. Do not rub your eyes after touching the cut flesh of the chile.

3 Heat the olive oil in a large, heavy-bottom skillet or ovenproof casserole until quite hot, then add the garlic and cook for 30 seconds. Add the shrimp, chile, paprika, and a pinch of salt and cook for 2–3 minutes, stirring all the time, until the shrimp turn pink and start to curl.

4 Serve the shrimp in the cooking dish, still sizzling. Accompany with toothpicks, to spear the shrimp, and chunks or slices of crusty bread to mop up the aromatic cooking oil.

crab tartlets

ingredients

makes 24

1 tbsp olive oil
1 small onion, finely chopped
1 garlic clove, finely chopped
splash of dry white wine
2 eggs
²/₃ cup milk or light cream
6 oz/175 g canned crabmeat,
    drained
¹/₂ cup grated Manchego
    or Parmesan cheese
2 tbsp chopped fresh
    flat-leaf parsley
pinch of freshly grated nutmeg
salt and pepper
sprigs of fresh dill, to garnish

pie dough

2¹/₄ cups all-purpose flour,
    plus extra for dusting
pinch of salt
³/₄ cup butter
2 tbsp cold water

method

1 To prepare the crabmeat filling, heat the olive oil in a heavy-bottom skillet, add the onion and cook for 5 minutes, or until softened but not browned. Add the garlic and cook for an additional 30 seconds. Add a splash of wine and cook for 1–2 minutes, or until most of the wine has evaporated.

2 Lightly whisk the eggs in a large mixing bowl, then whisk in the milk or cream. Add the crabmeat, cheese, and parsley, and the onion mixture. Season with nutmeg and salt and pepper to taste and mix well together.

3 To prepare the pie dough, mix the flour and salt together in a large mixing bowl. Add the butter, cut into small pieces, and rub in until the mixture resembles fine bread crumbs. Gradually stir in enough of the water to form a firm dough.

4 On a lightly floured counter, thinly roll out the dough. Using a plain, round 2³/₄-inch/7-cm cutter, cut the pastry into 24 circles. Use to line 24 x 1¹/₂-inch/4-cm tartlet pans. Carefully spoon the crabmeat mixture into the pastry shells, taking care not to overfill them. Bake in a preheated oven, 375°F/190°C, for 25–30 minutes, or until golden brown and set. Serve the crab tartlets hot or cold, garnished with fresh dill sprigs.

spanish spinach & tomato pizzas

ingredients

makes 32

2 tbsp olive oil, plus extra for
brushing and drizzling
1 onion, finely chopped
1 garlic clove, finely chopped
14 oz/400 g canned
chopped tomatoes
scant 3 cups baby spinach leaves
2 tbsp pine nuts
salt and pepper

bread dough

¼ cup warm water
½ tsp active dry yeast
pinch of sugar
1½ cups white bread flour,
plus extra for dusting
½ tsp salt

method

1 To make the bread dough, measure the water into
a small bowl, sprinkle in the yeast and sugar, and let
stand in a warm place for 10–15 minutes, or until frothy.

2 Sift the flour and salt into a large bowl. Make a well in
the center, pour in the yeast, then stir together. Work
the dough with your hands until it leaves the sides of
the bowl clean, then turn out onto a lightly floured
counter and knead for 10 minutes, or until smooth and
elastic. Put it in a clean bowl, cover with a damp dish
towel and let stand in a warm place for 1 hour, until
risen and doubled in size.

3 To make the topping, heat the olive oil in a large skillet.
Cook the onion until softened but not browned. Add
the garlic and cook for 30 seconds. Stir in the tomatoes
and cook until reduced to a thick sauce. Stir in the
spinach leaves until wilted. Season to taste.

4 Turn the risen dough out and knead well for 2–3
minutes. Roll out very thinly and, using a 2½-inch/6-cm
plain, round cutter, cut out 32 circles. Place on cookie
sheets brushed with olive oil. Cover each base with
the spinach mixture. Sprinkle with pine nuts and
drizzle over a little olive oil. Bake in a preheated oven,
400°F/200°C, for 10–15 minutes, or until the edges
of the dough are golden. Serve hot.

sautéed garlic mushrooms

ingredients

serves 6

1 lb/450 g button mushrooms
scant ⅓ cup olive oil
2 garlic cloves, finely chopped
squeeze of lemon juice
3 tbsp chopped fresh
    flat-leaf parsley
salt and pepper
crusty bread, to serve

method

1 Wipe or brush clean the mushrooms, then trim off the stalks close to the caps. Cut any large mushrooms in half or into fourths. Heat the olive oil in a large, heavy-bottom skillet, add the garlic and cook for 30 seconds–1 minute, or until lightly browned. Add the mushrooms and sauté over high heat, stirring most of the time, until the mushrooms have absorbed all the oil in the skillet.

2 Reduce the heat to low. When the juices have come out of the mushrooms, increase the heat again, and sauté for 4–5 minutes, stirring most of the time, until the juices have almost evaporated. Add a squeeze of lemon juice and season to taste with salt and pepper. Stir in the chopped parsley and cook for an additional minute.

3 Transfer the sautéed mushrooms to a warmed serving dish and serve piping hot or warm. Accompany with chunks or slices of crusty bread for mopping up the garlic cooking juices.

made with vegetables

simmered summer vegetables

ingredients

serves 6–8

1 large eggplant
1/4 cup olive oil
1 onion, thinly sliced
2 garlic cloves, finely chopped
2 zucchini, thinly sliced
1 red bell pepper, seeded and
    thinly sliced
1 green bell pepper, seeded
    and thinly sliced
8 tomatoes, peeled, seeded,
    and chopped
salt and pepper
chopped fresh flat-leaf parsley,
    to garnish
slices of thick country bread,
    to serve (optional)

method

1 Cut the eggplant into 1-inch/2.5-cm cubes. Heat the oil in a large ovenproof casserole, then add the onion and cook over medium heat, stirring occasionally, for 5 minutes, or until softened but not browned. Add the garlic to the casserole and cook, stirring, for 30 seconds, or until softened.

2 Increase the heat to medium–high, then add the eggplant cubes and cook, stirring occasionally, for 10 minutes, or until softened and beginning to brown. Add the zucchini and bell peppers and cook, stirring occasionally, for 10 minutes, or until softened. Add the tomatoes and season to taste with salt and pepper.

3 Bring the mixture to a boil, then reduce the heat, cover, and simmer, stirring occasionally so that the vegetables do not stick to the bottom of the pan, for 15–20 minutes, or until tender. If necessary, uncover, then increase the heat and cook to evaporate any excess liquid, as the mixture should be thick.

4 Serve hot or cold, garnished with chopped parsley and accompanied by bread slices, if using, for scooping up the vegetables.

patatas bravas

ingredients

serves 6

2 tbsp olive oil
1 onion, finely chopped
2 garlic cloves, crushed
¼ cup white wine or dry
   Spanish sherry
14 oz/400 g canned chopped
   tomatoes
2 tsp white or red wine vinegar
1–2 tsp crushed dried chiles
2 tsp hot or sweet smoked
   Spanish paprika
2 lb 4 oz/1 kg potatoes
olive oil, for pan-frying
salt

method

1 To make the sauce, heat the 2 tablespoons of oil in a
   pan, then add the onion and cook over medium heat,
   stirring occasionally, for 5 minutes, or until softened
   but not browned. Add the garlic and cook, stirring, for
   30 seconds. Add the wine and bring to a boil. Add the
   tomatoes, vinegar, chiles, and paprika, then reduce the
   heat and simmer, uncovered, for 10–15 minutes, or until
   a thick sauce forms.

2 When the sauce is cooked, use a handheld blender
   to blend until smooth. Alternatively, transfer the sauce
   to a food processor and process until smooth. Return
   the sauce to the pan and set aside.

3 Do not peel the potatoes, but cut them into chunky
   pieces. Heat enough oil in a large skillet to come about
   1 inch/2.5 cm up the side of the skillet. Add the potato
   pieces and cook over medium–high heat, turning
   occasionally, for 10–15 minutes, until golden brown
   and tender. Remove with a slotted spoon and drain
   on paper towels, then sprinkle with salt.

4 Meanwhile, gently reheat the sauce. Transfer the
   potatoes to a warmed serving dish and drizzle over
   the sauce. Serve hot, with wooden toothpicks to spear
   the potatoes.

fresh mint & bean pâté

ingredients

serves 12

1 lb 12 oz/800 g fresh fava beans
    in their pods, shelled to give
    about 12 oz/350 g
1 cup soft goat cheese
1 garlic clove, crushed
2 scallions, finely chopped
1 tbsp extra virgin olive oil,
    plus extra for serving
grated rind of 1 lemon and
    2 tbsp juice
about 60 large fresh mint leaves
salt and pepper
12 slices French bread, to serve

method

1 Cook the fava beans in a pan of boiling water for 8–10 minutes, or until tender. Drain well and let cool. When the beans are cool enough to handle, slip off their skins and put the beans in a food processor. This is a laborious task, but worth doing if you have the time. This quantity will take about 15 minutes to skin.

2 Add the goat cheese, garlic, scallions, oil, lemon rind and juice, and mint leaves to the fava beans and process until well mixed. Season the pâté to taste with salt and pepper. Turn into a bowl, cover, then let chill in the refrigerator for at least 1 hour before serving.

3 Preheat the broiler. To serve, toast the bread slices under a broiler until golden brown on both sides. Drizzle a little oil over the toasted bread slices, then spread the pâté on top and serve immediately.

pickled stuffed bell peppers

ingredients

serves 6

scant 1 cup Cuajada cheese,
Queso del Tietar, or other
fresh goat cheese
14 oz/400 g pickled sweet bell
peppers or pimientos del
piquillo, drained
1 tbsp finely chopped fresh dill
salt and pepper

method

1 Cut the cheese into pieces about ½ inch/1 cm long. Slit
the sides of the sweet bell peppers and seed, if you like.
Stuff the bell peppers with the cheese.

2 Arrange the stuffed bell peppers on serving plates.
Sprinkle with the dill and season to taste with salt and
pepper. Cover and let chill in the refrigerator until ready
to serve.

eggplant rolls

ingredients

serves 4

2 eggplants, thinly sliced
　　lengthwise
scant ⅓ cup olive oil, plus extra
　　for oiling
1 garlic clove, crushed
4 tbsp pesto
1½ cups grated mozzarella
basil leaves, torn into pieces
salt and pepper
fresh basil sprigs, to garnish

method

1 Sprinkle the eggplant slices liberally with salt and let
stand for 10–15 minutes to extract the bitter juices.
Turn the slices over and repeat. Rinse well with cold
water and drain on paper towels.

2 Heat the olive oil in a large skillet and add the garlic.
Fry the eggplant slices lightly on both sides, a few at
a time. Drain them on paper towels.

3 Spread the pesto onto one side of the eggplant slices.
Top with the grated mozzarella and sprinkle with the
torn basil leaves. Season with a little salt and pepper.
Roll up the slices and secure with wooden toothpicks.

4 Arrange the eggplant rolls in an oiled ovenproof
baking dish. Bake in a preheated oven, 350°F/180°C,
for 8–10 minutes.

5 Transfer the eggplant rolls to a warmed serving plate.
Scatter with the basil sprigs and serve at once.

roasted bell pepper salad

ingredients

serves 8

3 red bell peppers

3 yellow bell peppers

scant 1/3 cup extra virgin olive oil

2 tbsp dry sherry vinegar or
    lemon juice

2 garlic cloves, crushed

pinch of sugar

1 tbsp capers

8 small black Spanish olives

salt and pepper

2 tbsp chopped fresh marjoram,
    plus extra sprigs to garnish

method

1 Preheat the broiler. Place the bell peppers on a wire rack or broiler pan and cook under the broiler for 10 minutes, until their skins have blackened and blistered, turning them frequently.

2 Remove the roasted bell peppers from the heat, and either put them in a bowl and immediately cover tightly with a clean, damp dish towel, or put them in a plastic bag. The steam helps to soften the skins and makes it easier to remove them. Let the peppers stand for about 15 minutes, until they are cool enough to handle.

3 Holding one bell pepper at a time over a clean bowl, use a sharp knife to make a small hole in the base and gently squeeze out the juices and reserve them. Then, carefully peel off the blackened skin with your fingers or a knife and discard it. Cut the bell peppers in half and remove the stem, core, and seeds, then cut each bell pepper into neat thin strips. Arrange the bell pepper strips on a serving dish.

4 Add the olive oil, sherry vinegar, garlic, sugar, and salt and pepper to the reserved pepper juices. Whisk together until combined. Drizzle the dressing evenly over the salad. Sprinkle the capers, olives, and chopped marjoram over the salad, garnish with marjoram sprigs, and serve.

roasted bell peppers with honey & almonds

ingredients

serves 6

8 red bell peppers, cut into
    quarters and seeded
¼ cup olive oil
2 garlic cloves, thinly sliced
¼ cup flaked almonds
2 tbsp clear honey
2 tbsp sherry vinegar
2 tbsp chopped fresh parsley
salt and pepper

method

1 Preheat the broiler. Place the bell peppers, skin-side up, in a single layer on a cookie sheet. Cook under the hot broiler for 8–10 minutes, or until the skins have blistered and blackened. Using tongs, transfer to a plastic bag. Tie the top and let cool.

2 When the bell peppers are cool enough to handle, peel off the skin with your fingers or a knife and discard it. Chop the bell pepper flesh into bite-size pieces and place in a bowl.

3 Heat the olive oil in a large, heavy-bottom skillet. Add the garlic and cook over low heat, stirring frequently, for 4 minutes, or until golden. Stir in the almonds, honey, and vinegar, then pour the mixture over the bell pepper pieces. Add the parsley and season to taste with salt and pepper, then toss well.

4 Let cool to room temperature, then transfer to serving dishes. The bell peppers may also be covered and stored in the refrigerator, but should be returned to room temperature to serve.

stuffed bell peppers

ingredients

serves 6

6 tbsp olive oil, plus a little extra
　for rubbing on the bell peppers
2 onions, finely chopped
2 garlic cloves, crushed
²/₃ cup Spanish short-grain rice
¹/₃ cup raisins
¹/₃ cup pine nuts
generous ¹/₂ cup finely chopped
　fresh parsley
1 tbsp tomato paste, dissolved
　in 3 cups hot water
6 red, green, or yellow bell peppers
　(or a mix of colors)
salt and pepper

method

1 Heat the oil in a shallow, heavy-bottom flameproof casserole. Add the onions and cook for 3 minutes. Add the garlic and cook for an additional 2 minutes, or until the onion is soft but not brown.

2 Stir in the rice, raisins, and pine nuts until all are coated in the oil, then add half the parsley and salt and pepper to taste. Stir in the tomato paste mixture and bring to a boil. Reduce the heat and let simmer, uncovered, shaking the casserole frequently, for 20 minutes, or until the rice is tender, the liquid is absorbed, and small holes appear on the surface. Watch carefully because the raisins can catch and burn. Stir in the remaining parsley, then let cool slightly.

3 While the rice is simmering, cut the top off each bell pepper and reserve. Remove the core and seeds from each bell pepper.

4 Divide the stuffing equally among the bell peppers. Use wooden toothpicks to secure the tops back in place. Lightly rub each bell pepper with olive oil and arrange in a single layer in an ovenproof dish. Bake in a preheated oven, 400°F/200°C, for 30 minutes, or until the bell peppers are tender. Serve the bell peppers hot or let cool to room temperature.

baby potatoes with aïoli

ingredients

serves 6–8

1 quantity aïoli (see page 36)
1 lb/450 g baby new potatoes
1 tbsp chopped fresh
    flat-leaf parsley
salt

method

1 First, make the aïoli. For this recipe, the aïoli should be a little thinner so that it coats the potatoes when dipped. To ensure this, quickly blend in 1 tablespoon water so that it forms the consistency of a sauce. Set aside.

2 To prepare the potatoes, cut them in half or quarters to make bite-size pieces. If they are very small, you can leave them whole. Put the potatoes in a large pan of cold, salted water and bring to a boil. Lower the heat and let simmer for 7 minutes, or until just tender. Drain well, then turn out into a large bowl.

3 Transfer the potatoes with aïoli to a warmed serving dish, sprinkle over the parsley and salt to taste, and serve warm. Serve the aïoli separately, as a dipping sauce.

pan-fried potatoes with piquant paprika

ingredients

serves 6

3 tsp paprika

1 tsp ground cumin

$1/4$–$1/2$ tsp cayenne pepper

$1/2$ tsp salt

1 lb/450 g small old potatoes, peeled

corn oil, for pan-frying

sprigs of fresh flat-leaf parsley, to garnish

method

1 Put the paprika, cumin, cayenne pepper, and salt in a small bowl and mix well together. Set aside.

2 Cut each potato into 8 thick wedges. Pour corn oil into a large, heavy-bottom skillet to a depth of about 1 inch/2.5 cm. Heat the oil, then add the potato wedges, preferably in a single layer, and cook gently for 10 minutes, or until golden brown all over, turning from time to time. Remove from the skillet with a slotted spoon and let drain on paper towels.

3 Transfer the potato wedges to a large bowl and, while they are still hot, sprinkle with the paprika mixture, then gently toss them together to coat.

4 Turn the potatoes into a large, warmed serving dish, several smaller ones, or onto individual plates and serve hot, garnished with parsley sprigs.

warm potato salad

ingredients

serves 4–6

¾ cup olive oil
1 lb/450 g waxy potatoes,
    thinly sliced
¼ cup white wine vinegar
2 garlic cloves, finely chopped
salt and pepper

method

1 Heat ¼ cup of the olive oil in a large, heavy-bottom skillet. Add the potato slices and season to taste with salt, then cook over low heat, shaking the skillet occasionally, for 10 minutes. Turn the potatoes over and cook for an additional 5 minutes, or until tender but not browned.

2 Meanwhile, pour the vinegar into a small pan. Add the garlic and season to taste with pepper. Bring to a boil, then stir in the remaining olive oil.

3 Transfer the potatoes to a bowl and pour over the dressing. Toss gently and let stand for 15 minutes. Using a slotted spoon, transfer the potatoes to individual serving dishes and serve warm.

green beans with pine nuts

ingredients

serves 8

2 tbsp olive oil
scant ⅓ cup pine nuts
½–1 tsp paprika
1 lb/450 g green beans
1 small onion, finely chopped
1 garlic clove, finely chopped
juice of ½ lemon
salt and pepper

method

1 Heat the oil in a large, heavy-bottom skillet, add the pine nuts and cook for about 1 minute, stirring all the time and shaking the skillet, until light golden brown. Using a slotted spoon, remove the pine nuts from the skillet, drain well on paper towels, then transfer to a bowl. Set aside the oil in the skillet for later. Add the paprika, according to taste, to the pine nuts, stir together until coated, and then set aside.

2 Trim the green beans and remove any strings if necessary. Put the beans in a pan, pour over boiling water, return to a boil, and cook for 5 minutes, or until tender but still firm. Drain well in a strainer.

3 Reheat the oil in the skillet, add the onion and cook for 5–10 minutes, or until softened and starting to brown. Add the garlic and cook for an additional 30 seconds.

4 Add the beans to the skillet and cook for 2–3 minutes, tossing together with the onion until heated through. Season the beans to taste with salt and pepper.

5 Turn the contents of the skillet into a warmed serving dish, sprinkle over the lemon juice, and toss together. Sprinkle over the golden pine nuts and serve hot.

mixed beans & peas

ingredients

serves 4–6

6 oz/175 g shelled fresh
or frozen fava beans
4 oz/115 g fresh or frozen
green beans
4 oz/115 g snow peas
1 shallot, finely chopped
6 fresh mint sprigs
¼ cup olive oil
1 tbsp sherry vinegar
1 garlic clove, finely chopped
salt and pepper

method

1 Bring a large pan of lightly salted water to a boil. Add
the fava beans and reduce the heat, then cover and
simmer for 7 minutes. Remove the beans with a slotted
spoon, then plunge into cold water and drain. Remove
and discard the outer skins.

2 Meanwhile, return the pan of salted water to a boil.
Add the green beans and return to a boil again. Drain
and refresh under cold running water. Drain well.

3 Mix the fava beans, green beans, snow peas, and
shallot together in a bowl. Strip the leaves from the
mint sprigs, then reserve half and add the remainder
to the bean mixture. Finely chop the reserved mint.

4 Whisk the olive oil, vinegar, garlic, and chopped mint
together in a separate bowl and season to taste with
salt and pepper. Pour the dressing over the bean
mixture and toss lightly to coat. Cover with plastic
wrap and let chill in the refrigerator until required.

garlic tomatoes

ingredients

serves 6

8 deep red tomatoes
3 fresh thyme sprigs, plus extra
    to garnish
12 garlic cloves, unpeeled
scant ⅓ cup olive oil
salt and pepper

method

1 Cut the tomatoes in half lengthwise and arrange, cut-side up, in a single layer in a large, ovenproof dish. Tuck the thyme sprigs and garlic cloves between them.

2 Drizzle the olive oil all over the tomatoes and season to taste with pepper. Bake in a preheated oven, 425°F/220°C, for 40–45 minutes, or until the tomatoes are softened and beginning to char slightly around the edges.

3 Remove and discard the thyme sprigs. Season the tomatoes to taste with salt and pepper. Garnish with the extra thyme sprigs and serve hot or warm. Squeeze the pulp from the garlic over the tomatoes at the table.

baked tomato nests

ingredients

serves 4

4 large ripe tomatoes
4 large eggs
¼ cup heavy cream
generous 1 cup grated mature
    Mahon, Manchego, or
    Parmesan cheese
salt and pepper

method

1 Cut a slice off the top of the tomatoes, and using a teaspoon, carefully scoop out the pulp and seeds without piercing the shells. Turn the tomato shells upside down on paper towels and let drain for 15 minutes. Season the insides of the shells with salt and pepper.

2 Place the tomatoes in an ovenproof dish just large enough to hold them in a single layer. Carefully break 1 egg into each tomato shell, then top with 1 tablespoon of cream and 1 tablespoon of grated cheese.

3 Bake in a preheated oven, 350°F/180°C, for 15–20 minutes, or until the eggs are just set. Serve hot.

artichoke hearts & asparagus

ingredients

serves 4–6

1 lb/450 g asparagus spears
14 oz/400 g canned artichoke
    hearts, drained and rinsed
2 tbsp freshly squeezed
    orange juice
½ tsp finely grated
    orange rind
2 tbsp walnut oil
1 tsp Dijon mustard
salt and pepper
salad greens, to serve

method

1 Trim and discard the coarse, woody ends of the
asparagus spears. Make sure all the stems are about
the same length, then tie them together loosely with
clean kitchen string. If you have an asparagus steamer,
just place them directly in the basket.

2 Bring a tall pan of lightly salted water to a boil. Add
the asparagus, making sure that the tips are protruding
above the water, then reduce the heat and let simmer
for 10–15 minutes, or until tender. Test by piercing
a stem just above the water level with the point of
a sharp knife. Drain, then refresh under cold running
water and drain again.

3 Cut the asparagus spears into 1-inch/2.5-cm pieces,
keeping the tips intact. Cut the artichoke hearts into
small wedges and combine with the asparagus in
a bowl.

4 Whisk the orange juice, orange rind, walnut oil, and
mustard together in a bowl and season to taste with
salt and pepper. If serving immediately, pour the
dressing over the artichoke hearts and asparagus and
toss lightly.

5 Arrange the salad greens in individual serving dishes
and top with the artichoke and asparagus mixture.
Serve immediately.

stuffed mushrooms

ingredients

serves 6

¾ cup butter
4 garlic cloves, finely chopped
6 large open mushrooms,
    stems removed
1 cup fresh white breadcrumbs
1 tbsp chopped fresh thyme
1 egg, lightly beaten
salt and pepper

method

1 Cream the butter in a bowl until softened, then beat in the garlic. Divide two-thirds of the garlic butter between the mushroom caps and arrange them, cup-side up, on a cookie sheet.

2 Melt the remaining garlic butter in a heavy-bottom or nonstick skillet. Add the breadcrumbs and cook over low heat, stirring frequently, until golden. Remove from the heat and tip into a bowl. Stir in the thyme and season to taste with salt and pepper. Stir in the beaten egg until thoroughly combined.

3 Divide the breadcrumb mixture among the mushroom caps and bake in a preheated oven, 350°F/180°C, for 15 minutes, or until the stuffing is golden brown and the mushrooms are tender. Serve hot or warm.

marinated eggplants

ingredients

serves 4

2 eggplants, halved lengthwise
¼ cup olive oil
2 garlic cloves, finely chopped
2 tbsp chopped fresh parsley
1 tbsp chopped fresh thyme
2 tbsp lemon juice
salt and pepper

method

1 Make three slashes in the flesh of the eggplant halves and place, cut-side down, in an ovenproof dish. Season to taste with salt and pepper, then pour over the olive oil and sprinkle with the garlic, parsley, and thyme. Cover and let marinate at room temperature for 2–3 hours.

2 Uncover the dish and roast the eggplants in a preheated oven, 350°F/180°C, for 45 minutes. Remove the dish from the oven and turn the eggplants over. Baste with the cooking juices and sprinkle with the lemon juice. Return to the oven and cook for an additional 15 minutes.

3 Transfer the eggplants to serving plates. Spoon over the cooking juices and serve hot or warm.

charbroiled leeks

ingredients

serves 4

8 baby leeks
2 tbsp olive oil, plus extra
　　for brushing
2 tbsp white wine vinegar
2 tbsp snipped fresh chives
2 tbsp chopped fresh parsley
1 tsp Dijon mustard
salt and pepper
sprigs of fresh parsley,
　　to garnish

method

1 Trim the leeks and halve lengthwise. Rinse well to remove any grit and pat dry with paper towels.

2 Heat a grill pan and brush with olive oil. Add the leeks and cook over medium–high heat, turning occasionally, for 5 minutes. Transfer to a shallow dish.

3 Meanwhile, whisk the olive oil, vinegar, chives, parsley, and mustard together in a bowl and season to taste with salt and pepper. Pour over the leeks, turning to coat. Cover with plastic wrap and let marinate at room temperature, turning occasionally, for 30 minutes.

4 Divide the leeks among individual serving plates, then garnish with parsley sprigs and serve.

orange & fennel salad

ingredients

serves 4

4 large, juicy oranges
1 large fennel bulb, very
 thinly sliced
1 mild white onion,
 finely sliced
2 tbsp extra virgin olive oil
12 plump black olives, pitted
 and thinly sliced
1 fresh red chile, seeded and very
 thinly sliced (optional)
finely chopped fresh parsley,
 to garnish
French bread, to serve

method

1 Finely grate the rind from the oranges into a bowl and reserve. Using a small, serrated knife, remove all the white pith from the oranges, working over a bowl to catch the juices. Cut the oranges horizontally into thin slices.

2 Toss the orange slices with the fennel and onion slices. Whisk the olive oil into the reserved orange juice, then spoon over the oranges. Sprinkle the olive slices over the top, add the chile, if using, then sprinkle with the orange rind and parsley. Serve with slices of French bread.

tomato & olive salad

ingredients

serves 6

2 tbsp sherry or red wine vinegar

scant ⅓ cup olive oil

1 garlic clove, finely chopped

1 tsp paprika

4 tomatoes, peeled and diced

12 anchovy-stuffed or
    pimiento-stuffed olives

½ cucumber, peeled and diced

2 shallots, finely chopped

1 tbsp pickled capers in brine,
    drained

2–3 chicory heads, separated
    into leaves

salt

method

1 To make the dressing, whisk the vinegar, olive oil, garlic, and paprika together in a bowl. Season to taste with salt and reserve.

2 Place the tomatoes, olives, cucumber, shallots, and capers in a separate bowl. Pour over the dressing and toss lightly.

3 Line six individual serving bowls with chicory leaves. Spoon an equal quantity of the salad into the center of each and serve.

for meat lovers

calves' liver in almond saffron sauce

ingredients

serves 6

¼ cup olive oil
2 slices white bread
⅔ cup blanched almonds
2 garlic cloves, crushed
pinch of saffron strands
⅔ cup dry Spanish sherry
    or white wine
1¼ cups vegetable stock
1 lb/450 g calves' liver
all-purpose flour, for dusting
salt and pepper
chopped fresh flat-leaf parsley,
    to garnish
crusty bread, to serve

method

1 To make the sauce, heat 2 tablespoons of the oil in a large skillet. Tear the bread into small pieces and add to the skillet with the almonds. Cook over low heat, stirring frequently, for 2 minutes, or until golden brown. Stir in the garlic and cook, stirring, for 30 seconds.

2 Add the saffron and sherry to the skillet and season to taste with salt and pepper. Bring to a boil and continue to boil for 1–2 minutes. Remove from the heat and let cool slightly, then transfer the mixture to a food processor. Add the stock and process until smooth. Set aside.

3 Cut the liver into large bite-size pieces. Dust lightly with flour and season generously with pepper. Heat the remaining oil in the skillet, then add the liver and cook over medium heat, stirring constantly, for 2–3 minutes, or until firm and lightly browned.

4 Pour the sauce into the skillet and reheat gently for 1–2 minutes. Transfer to a warmed serving dish and garnish with chopped parsley. Serve hot, accompanied by chunks of crusty bread to mop up the sauce.

chorizo bread pockets

ingredients

serves 4

scant 1½ cups white bread flour,
  plus extra for dusting
1½ tsp active dry yeast
½ tsp salt
¼ tsp superfine sugar
½ cup warm water
sunflower oil, for oiling
4 oz/115 g chorizo sausage,
  outer casing removed, cut into
  16 equal-sized chunks

method.

1 To make the bread dough, put the flour, yeast, salt, and sugar in a large bowl and make a well in the center. Pour the water into the well and gradually mix in the flour from the side. Mix together to form a soft dough.

2 Turn the dough onto a lightly floured counter and knead for 10 minutes, or until smooth and elastic and no longer sticky. Shape the dough into a ball and put in a clean bowl. Cover with a clean, damp dish towel and leave in a warm place for 1 hour, or until the dough has risen and doubled in size.

3 Lightly oil a cookie sheet. Turn out the risen dough onto a lightly floured counter and knead lightly for 2–3 minutes to knock out the air.

4 Divide the dough into 16 equal-size pieces. Shape each piece into a ball and roll out on a lightly floured counter to a 4½-inch/12-cm circle. Put a piece of chorizo on each circle and gather the dough at the top, enclosing the chorizo, then pinch the edges together to seal. Put each dough pocket, pinched-side down, on the prepared cookie sheet.

5 Bake in a preheated oven, 400°F/200°C, for 20 minutes, or until pale golden brown. Turn the pockets over so that the pinched ends are facing up and arrange in a serving basket.

fried chorizo with herbs

ingredients

serves 6–8

1 lb 9 oz/700 g chorizo
    cooking sausage
2 tbsp olive oil
2 garlic cloves, finely chopped
3 tbsp chopped mixed
    fresh herbs

method

1 Using a sharp knife, cut the chorizo into ¼-inch/5-mm thick slices. Heat a large, heavy-bottom skillet. Add the chorizo slices, without any additional fat, and cook over medium heat, stirring frequently, for 5 minutes, or until crisp and browned.

2 Remove the chorizo slices with a spatula or slotted spoon and drain well on paper towels. Drain the fat from the skillet and wipe out with paper towels.

3 Heat the olive oil in the skillet over a medium–low heat. Add the chorizo slices, garlic, and herbs and cook, stirring occasionally, until heated through. Serve the chorizo immediately.

variation

Green and yellow bell peppers fried with the chorizo sausage make a colorful addition to this dish.

chickpeas & chorizo

ingredients

serves 4–6

9 oz/250 g chorizo sausage in
    1 piece, outer casing removed

¼ cup olive oil

1 onion, finely chopped

1 large garlic clove, crushed

14 oz/400 g canned chickpeas,
    drained and rinsed

6 pimientos del piquillo, drained,
    patted dry, and sliced

1 tbsp sherry vinegar,
    or to taste

salt and pepper

finely chopped fresh parsley,
    to garnish

crusty bread slices, to serve

method

1 Cut the chorizo into ½-inch/1-cm dice. Heat the oil in a heavy-bottom skillet over medium heat, then add the onion and garlic. Cook, stirring occasionally, until the onion is softened but not browned. Stir in the chorizo and cook until heated through.

2 Tip the mixture into a bowl and stir in the chickpeas and pimientos. Splash with sherry vinegar and season to taste with salt and pepper. Serve hot or at room temperature, generously sprinkled with parsley, with plenty of crusty bread.

chorizo & mushroom kabobs

ingredients

makes 25

2 tbsp olive oil

25 pieces chorizo sausage, each about ½-inch/1-cm square (about 3½ oz/100 g)

25 button mushrooms, wiped and stems removed

1 green bell pepper, broiled, peeled, and cut into 25 squares

method

1 Heat the olive oil in a skillet over medium heat. Add the chorizo pieces and cook them for about 20 seconds, stirring.

2 Add the mushrooms and continue cooking for an additional 1–2 minutes, until the mushrooms begin to brown and absorb the fat in the skillet.

3 Thread a bell pepper square, a piece of chorizo, and a mushroom onto a wooden toothpick. Continue until all the ingredients are used. Serve the kabobs hot or at room temperature.

chorizo in red wine

ingredients

serves 6

7 oz/200 g chorizo sausage
generous ¾ cup Spanish red wine
2 tbsp brandy (optional)
fresh flat-leaf parsley sprigs,
    to garnish
crusty bread, to serve

method

1 Using a fork, prick the chorizo in three or four places and pour the wine over. Place the chorizo and wine in a large pan. Bring the wine to a boil, then reduce the heat and simmer gently, covered, for 15–20 minutes. Transfer the chorizo and wine to a bowl or dish, cover and let the sausage marinate in the wine for 8 hours or overnight.

2 Remove the chorizo from the bowl or dish and reserve the wine. Remove the outer casing from the chorizo and cut the sausage into ¼-inch/5-mm slices. Place the slices in a large, heavy-bottom skillet or flameproof serving dish.

3 If you are adding the brandy, pour it into a small pan and heat gently. Pour the brandy over the chorizo slices, then stand well back and set alight. When the flames have died down, shake the pan gently and add the reserved wine to the pan, then cook the chorizo over high heat until almost all of the wine has evaporated.

4 Serve the chorizo in red wine piping hot, in the dish in which it was cooked, sprinkled with parsley to garnish. Accompany with chunks or slices of bread to mop up the juices and provide wooden toothpicks to spear the pieces of chorizo.

fava beans with serrano ham

ingredients

serves 6–8

2 oz/55 g Serrano or prosciutto
ham, pancetta, or rindless
smoked lean bacon

4 oz/115 g chorizo sausage,
outer casing removed

4 tbsp olive oil

1 onion, finely chopped

2 garlic cloves, finely chopped

splash of dry white wine

1 lb/450 g frozen fava beans,
thawed, or about 3 lb/1.3 kg
fresh fava beans in their pods,
shelled to give 1 lb/450 g

1 tbsp chopped fresh mint or dill,
plus extra to garnish

pinch of sugar

salt and pepper

method

1 Using a sharp knife, cut the ham, pancetta, or bacon into small strips. Cut the chorizo into ³/₄-inch/2-cm cubes. Heat the olive oil in a large, heavy-bottom skillet or flameproof dish that has a lid. Add the onion and cook for 5 minutes, or until softened and starting to brown. If you are using pancetta or bacon, add it with the onion. Add the garlic and cook for 30 seconds.

2 Pour the wine into the skillet, increase the heat, and let it bubble to evaporate the alcohol, then lower the heat. Add the fava beans, ham, if using, and the chorizo and cook for 1–2 minutes, stirring all the time to coat in the oil.

3 Cover the skillet and let the beans simmer very gently in the oil, stirring from time to time, for 10–15 minutes, or until the beans are tender. It may be necessary to add a little water to the skillet during cooking, so keep an eye on it and add a splash if the beans appear to become too dry. Stir in the mint or dill and sugar. Season the dish with salt and pepper, but taste first as you may find that it does not need any salt.

4 Transfer the fava beans to a large, warmed serving dish, several smaller ones, or individual plates and serve piping hot, garnished with chopped mint or dill.

serrano ham with arugula

ingredients

serves 6

5 oz/140 g arugula, separated
    into leaves
scant ⅓ cup olive oil
1½ tbsp orange juice
10 oz/280 g thinly sliced
    Serrano ham
salt and pepper

method

1 Place the arugula in a bowl and pour in the olive oil
   and orange juice. Season to taste with salt and pepper
   and toss well.

2 Arrange the slices of ham on individual serving plates,
   folding it into attractive shapes. Divide the arugula
   between the plates and serve immediately.

variation

Try adding 1 cup of feta cheese and a handful of
black olives to this dish. Replace the orange juice with
a tablespoon of honey, if preferred.

tiny meatballs with tomato sauce

ingredients

makes 60

olive oil
1 red onion, very finely chopped
1 lb 2 oz/500 g fresh
    ground lamb
1 large egg, beaten
2 tsp freshly squeezed
    lemon juice
½ tsp ground cumin
pinch of cayenne pepper,
    to taste
2 tbsp very finely chopped
    fresh mint
salt and pepper

tomato sauce

¼ cup olive oil
10 large garlic cloves
5 oz/140 g scallions, chopped
4 large red bell peppers,
    seeded and chopped
2 lb 4 oz/1 kg ripe, fresh
    tomatoes, chopped
2 thin strips freshly pared
    orange rind
salt and pepper

method

1 To make the tomato sauce, heat the olive oil in a heavy-bottom pan over medium heat. Add the garlic, scallions, and bell peppers and cook for 10 minutes, until the peppers are soft but not brown. Add the tomatoes and orange rind. Add salt and pepper to taste and bring to a boil. Reduce the heat and cook, uncovered, for 45 minutes, until the sauce thickens. Set aside until the meatballs are prepared.

2 Heat 1 tablespoon of olive oil in a skillet over medium heat. Add the onion and cook for 5 minutes, stirring occasionally, until softened but not browned. Remove the skillet from the heat and let cool. Add the onion to the lamb with the egg, lemon juice, cumin, cayenne, mint, and salt and pepper to taste in a large bowl. Use your hands to squeeze all the ingredients together.

3 With wet hands, shape the mixture into about sixty ¾-inch/2-cm balls. Place on a tray and let chill in the refrigerator for at least 20 minutes.

4 When ready to cook, heat a small amount of olive oil in one or two large skillets. Arrange the meatballs in a single layer, and cook over medium heat for 5 minutes, until brown on the outside but still slightly pink inside.

5 Gently reheat the tomato and serve with the meatballs for dipping.

mixed tapas platter with beef

ingredients

serves 8–10

7 oz/200 g small waxy potatoes, unpeeled

scant ⅓ cup olive oil

2 sirloin steaks, about 8 oz/225 g each

1 fresh red chile, seeded and finely chopped (optional)

12 oz/350 g Queso del Montsec or other goat cheese, sliced

6 oz/175 g mixed salad greens

2 tbsp black olives

2 tbsp green olives

2 oz/55 g canned anchovies in oil, drained and halved lengthwise

1 tbsp capers, drained and rinsed

salt and pepper

method

1 Cook the potatoes in a pan of lightly salted boiling water for 15–20 minutes, or until just tender. Drain and let cool slightly.

2 Heat a heavy-bottom skillet or grill pan over high heat and brush with 1 tablespoon of the olive oil. Season the steaks to taste with pepper and add to the pan. Cook for 1–1½ minutes on each side, or until browned. Reduce the heat to medium and cook the steaks for 1½ minutes on each side. Remove and rest the steaks for 10–15 minutes.

3 Heat 2 tablespoons of the remaining oil in a skillet. Add the chile, if using, and the potatoes and cook, turning frequently, for 10 minutes, or until crisp and golden.

4 Thinly slice the steaks and arrange the slices alternately with the cheese slices along the sides of a serving platter. Mix the salad greens, olives, anchovies, and capers together, then arrange along the center of the platter. Drizzle with the remaining oil, then top with the potatoes. Serve warm or at room temperature.

beef skewers with orange & garlic

ingredients

serves 6–8

3 tbsp white wine
2 tbsp olive oil
3 garlic cloves, finely chopped
juice of 1 orange
1 lb/450 g rump steak, cubed
1 lb/450 g baby onions, halved
2 orange bell peppers, seeded
and cut into squares
8 oz/225 g cherry tomatoes,
halved
salt and pepper

method

1 Mix the wine, olive oil, garlic, and orange juice together in a shallow, nonmetallic dish. Add the cubes of steak, season to taste with salt and pepper, and toss to coat. Cover with plastic wrap and let marinate in the refrigerator for 2–8 hours.

2 Soak several wooden small skewers in cold water for 30 minutes before using. Preheat the broiler to high. Drain the steak, reserving the marinade. Thread the steak, onions, bell peppers, and tomatoes alternately onto the skewers.

3 Preheat the broiler to high. Cook the skewers under the hot broiler, turning and brushing frequently with the marinade, for 10 minutes, or until cooked through. Transfer to warmed serving plates and serve immediately.

citrus lamb skewers

ingredients

serves 8

2 garlic cloves,
   finely chopped
1 Spanish onion, finely chopped
2 tsp finely grated lemon rind
2 tbsp lemon juice
1 tsp fresh thyme leaves
1 tsp ground coriander
1 tsp ground cumin
2 tbsp red wine vinegar
½ cup olive oil
2 lb 4 oz/1 kg lamb fillet, cut
   into ¾-inch/2-cm pieces
orange or lemon slices,
   to garnish

method

1 Mix the garlic, onion, lemon rind, lemon juice, thyme, coriander, cumin, vinegar, and olive oil together in a large, shallow, nonmetallic dish, whisking the marinade well until thoroughly combined.

2 Soak the wooden skewers in cold water for 30 minutes before using. Thread the pieces of lamb onto the skewers and add to the dish, turning well to coat. Cover with plastic wrap and let marinate in the refrigerator for 2–8 hours, turning occasionally.

3 Drain the skewers, reserving the marinade. Cook the skewers under the hot broiler, turning frequently and brushing with the marinade, for 10 minutes, or until tender and cooked to your liking. Serve immediately, garnished with orange slices.

miniature pork brochettes

ingredients

makes 12

1 lb/450 g lean boneless pork
3 tbsp olive oil, plus extra for
    oiling (optional)
grated rind and juice of
    1 large lemon
2 garlic cloves, crushed
2 tbsp chopped fresh
    flat-leaf parsley,
    plus extra to garnish
1 tbsp ras-el-hanout
    spice blend
salt and pepper

method

1 Cut the pork into pieces about ¾ inch/2 cm square and put in a large, shallow, nonmetallic dish that will hold the pieces in a single layer.

2 To prepare the marinade, put the remaining ingredients in a bowl and mix well together. Pour the marinade over the pork and toss the meat in it until well coated. Cover the dish and let marinate in the refrigerator for 8 hours or overnight, stirring the pork 2–3 times.

3 Soak the wooden skewers in cold water for 30 minutes before using. Preheat the broiler, grill pan, or barbecue. Thread 3 marinated pork pieces, leaving a little space between each piece, onto each skewer. Cook the brochettes for 10–15 minutes, or until tender and lightly charred, turning several times and basting with the remaining marinade during cooking. Serve the pork brochettes piping hot, garnished with parsley.

chicken livers in sherry sauce

ingredients

serves 6

1 lb/450 g chicken livers
2 tbsp olive oil
1 small onion, finely chopped
2 garlic cloves, finely chopped
generous ⅓ cup dry Spanish sherry
2 tbsp chopped fresh
    flat-leaf parsley
salt and pepper
crusty bread or toast, to serve

method

1 If necessary, first trim the chicken livers, cutting away any ducts and gristle, then cut them into small, bite-size pieces.

2 Heat the olive oil in a large, heavy-bottom skillet. Add the onion and cook for 5 minutes, or until softened but not browned. Add the garlic to the skillet and cook for an additional 30 seconds.

3 Add the chicken livers to the skillet and cook for 2–3 minutes, stirring all the time, until they are firm and have changed color on the outside but are still pink and soft in the center. Using a slotted spoon, lift the chicken livers from the pan, transfer them to a large, warmed serving dish and keep warm.

4 Add the sherry to the skillet, increase the heat, and let it bubble for 3–4 minutes to evaporate the alcohol and reduce slightly. At the same time, deglaze the skillet by scraping and stirring all the bits on the bottom of the skillet into the sauce with a wooden spoon. Season the sauce to taste with salt and pepper.

5 Pour the sherry sauce over the chicken livers and sprinkle over the parsley. Serve piping hot, with chunks or slices of crusty bread or toast to mop up the sherry sauce.

chicken rolls with olives

ingredients

serves 6–8

²/₃ cup black olives in oil, drained reserving 2 tbsp oil
generous ½ cup butter, softened
3 tbsp chopped fresh parsley
4 skinless, boneless chicken breasts

method

1 Pit and chop the olives. Mix half the olives, the butter, and parsley together in a bowl.

2 Place the chicken breasts between two sheets of plastic wrap and beat gently with a meat mallet or the side of a rolling pin.

3 Spread the olive and herb butter over one side of each flattened chicken breast and roll up. Secure with a wooden toothpick or tie with clean string if necessary to keep in place.

4 Place the chicken rolls in an ovenproof dish. Drizzle over the oil from the olive jar and bake in a preheated oven, 400°F/200°C, for 45–55 minutes, or until tender and the juices run clear when the chicken is pierced with the point of a sharp knife.

5 Transfer the chicken rolls to a cutting board and discard the toothpicks or string. Using a sharp knife, cut into slices, then transfer to warmed serving plates. Scatter over the remaining olives and serve.

chicken in lemon & garlic

ingredients

serves 6–8

4 large skinless, boneless
   chicken breasts
scant ⅓ cup olive oil
1 onion, finely chopped
6 garlic cloves, finely chopped
grated rind of 1 lemon,
   zest of 1 lemon and juice
   of both lemons
3 tbsp chopped fresh flat-leaf
   parsley, plus extra
   to garnish
salt and pepper
lemon wedges and crusty bread,
   to serve

method

1 Using a sharp knife, slice the chicken breasts widthwise into very thin slices. Heat the olive oil in a large, heavy-bottom skillet, add the onion and cook for 5 minutes, or until softened but not browned. Add the garlic and cook for an additional 30 seconds.

2 Add the sliced chicken to the skillet and cook gently for 5–10 minutes, stirring from time to time, until all the ingredients are lightly browned and the chicken is tender.

3 Add the grated lemon rind and the lemon juice and let it bubble. At the same time, deglaze the skillet by scraping and stirring all the bits on the bottom of the skillet into the juices with a wooden spoon. Remove the skillet from the heat, stir in the parsley, and season to taste with salt and pepper.

4 Transfer, piping hot, to a warmed serving dish. Sprinkle with the lemon zest, garnish with the parsley, and serve with lemon wedges for squeezing over the chicken, accompanied by chunks or slices of crusty bread for mopping up the juices.

for seafood fans

salt cod fritters with spinach

ingredients

makes 16

9 oz/250 g pre-soaked salt
      cod in 1 piece
2 lemon slices
2 fresh parsley sprigs
1 bay leaf
½ tbsp garlic-flavored olive oil
3 oz/85 g fresh baby spinach,
      rinsed
¼ tsp smoked sweet, mild, or hot
      Spanish paprika, to taste
olive oil, for frying
coarse sea salt (optional)
dipping sauce, for serving
      (optional)

batter

1 cup all-purpose flour
1 tsp baking powder
¼ tsp salt
1 large egg, lightly beaten
⅔ cup milk

method

1 To make the batter, sift the flour, baking powder, and
   salt into a large bowl and make a well. Mix the egg with
   the milk and pour into the well in the flour, stirring to
   make a smooth batter with a thick coating consistency.
   Let stand for at least 1 hour.

2 Transfer the cod to a large skillet. Add the lemon slices,
   parsley sprigs, bay leaf, and enough water to cover and
   bring to a boil. Reduce the heat and simmer for 30–45
   minutes, or until the fish is tender and flakes easily.

3 Meanwhile, heat the garlic-flavored olive oil in a small
   pan over medium heat. Add the spinach and cook for
   3–4 minutes, or until wilted. Drain and finely chop the
   spinach, then stir it into the batter with the paprika.

4 Remove the fish from the water and flake the flesh
   into pieces, removing all the skin and tiny bones. Stir
   the fish into the batter.

5 Heat 2-inch/5-cm of olive oil in a heavy-bottom skillet
   to 350–375°F/180–190°C, or until a cube of bread
   browns in 30 seconds. Use a greased tablespoon or
   measuring spoon to drop spoonfuls of the batter into
   the oil, then cook for 8–10 minutes, until golden brown.
   Work in batches to avoid crowding the skillet. Transfer
   the fritters to paper towels to drain and sprinkle with
   sea salt, if using. Serve hot with a dipping sauce, if liked.

salmon with red bell pepper sauce

ingredients

serves 6

2 red bell peppers
¼ cup olive oil
1 onion, coarsely chopped
1 garlic clove, finely chopped
⅓ cup dry white wine
generous ⅓ cup heavy cream
1 lb 9 oz/700 g salmon fillets,
    skinned and cut into cubes
salt and pepper
chopped fresh flat-leaf parsley,
    for garnish

method

1 Brush the red bell peppers with 2 teaspoons of the oil and put in a roasting pan. Roast in a preheated oven, 400°F/200°C, for 30 minutes. Turn over and roast for an additional 10 minutes, or until the skins are blackened.

2 Heat 2 tablespoons of the remaining oil in a large skillet, then add the onion and cook for 5 minutes, or until softened. Add the garlic and cook for 30 seconds, or until softened. Add the wine and bring to a boil for 1 minute. Remove from the heat and set aside.

3 When the bell peppers are cooked, transfer to a plastic bag, and let cool. Using a sharp knife or your fingers, carefully peel away the skin from the bell peppers. Halve, core, and seed the bell peppers and put the flesh in a food processor. Add the onion mixture and cream to the bell peppers and process to a smooth purée. Season to taste with salt and pepper. Pour into a pan.

4 Heat the remaining oil in the skillet, add the salmon cubes and cook, turning occasionally, for 8–10 minutes, or until cooked through and golden brown on both sides. Meanwhile, gently heat the sauce in the pan.

5 Transfer the cooked salmon to a warmed serving dish. Drizzle over some of the bell pepper sauce and serve the remaining sauce in a small serving bowl. Serve hot, garnished with chopped parsley.

saffron shrimp with lemon mayonnaise

ingredients

serves 6–8

2 lb 12 oz/1.25 kg raw
jumbo shrimp
generous ½ cup all-purpose flour
½ cup light beer
2 tbsp olive oil
pinch of saffron powder
2 egg whites
vegetable oil, for deep-frying

lemon mayonnaise

4 garlic cloves
2 egg yolks
1 tbsp lemon juice
1 tbsp finely grated lemon rind
1¼ cups corn oil
salt and pepper

method

1 To make the mayonnaise, place the garlic cloves on a cutting board and sprinkle with a little sea salt, and finely chop. Transfer to a food processor or blender and add the egg yolks, lemon juice, and lemon rind. Process briefly until just blended. Add the corn oil until it is fully incorporated. Scrape the mayonnaise into a serving bowl, season to taste with salt and pepper, then cover and let chill until ready to serve.

2 Pull the heads off the shrimp and peel, leaving the tails intact. Cut along the length of the back of each shrimp and remove and discard the dark vein. Rinse under cold running water and pat dry with kitchen towels.

3 Sift the flour into a bowl. Mix the beer, oil, and saffron together in a pitcher, then whisk into the flour. Cover and let stand for 30 minutes to rest. Whisk the egg whites in a spotlessly clean, greasefree bowl until stiff. Gently fold the egg whites into the flour mixture.

4 Heat the vegetable oil in a deep-fat fryer to 350–375°F/ 180–190°C. Dip the shrimp into the batter and shake off any excess. Add the shrimp to the oil and deep-fry for 2–3 minutes, or until crisp. Remove and drain on kitchen towels. Serve immediately with the mayonnaise.

mussels in a vinaigrette dressing

ingredients

serves 6

⅓ cup extra virgin olive oil
2 tbsp white wine vinegar
1 shallot, finely chopped
1 garlic clove, crushed
2 tbsp capers, chopped
1 fresh red chile, seeded and
    finely chopped (optional)
2 lb 4 oz/1 kg live mussels,
    in their shells
⅓ cup dry white wine
3 tbsp chopped fresh flat-leaf
    parsley
salt and pepper
crusty bread, to serve (optional)

method

1 To make the dressing, put the oil and vinegar in a bowl and whisk together. Stir in the shallot, garlic, capers, and chile, if using. Season to taste with salt and pepper.

2 Clean the mussels by scrubbing or scraping the shells and pulling out any beards that are attached to them. Discard any with broken shells or any that refuse to close when tapped. Put the mussels in a colander and rinse well under cold running water.

3 Put the mussels in a large pan and add the wine. Bring to a boil, then cover and cook over high heat, shaking the pan occasionally, for 3–4 minutes, or until the mussels have opened. Drain the mussels, discarding any that remain closed, and let cool.

4 When the mussels are cool enough to handle, discard the empty half-shells and arrange the mussels, in their other half-shells, in a large, shallow serving dish. Discard any mussels that remain closed. Whisk the dressing again and spoon over the mussels. Cover and chill in the refrigerator for at least 1 hour.

5 To serve, sprinkle the parsley over the top and serve with crusty bread, if using, to mop up the dressing.

clams in tomato & garlic sauce

ingredients

serves 6-8

2 hard-cooked eggs, cooled,
　shelled, and halved lengthwise
3 tbsp olive oil
1 Spanish onion, chopped
2 garlic cloves, finely chopped
1 lb 9 oz/700 g tomatoes, peeled
　and diced
¾ cup fresh white breadcrumbs
2 lb 4 oz/1 kg fresh clams
generous 1¼ cups dry white wine
2 tbsp chopped fresh parsley
salt and pepper
lemon wedges, for garnish

method

1 Scoop out the egg yolks using a teaspoon and rub
　through a fine strainer into a bowl. Chop the whites
　and reserve separately.

2 Heat the olive oil in a large, heavy-bottom skillet. Add
　the onion and cook over low heat, stirring occasionally,
　for 5 minutes, or until softened. Add the garlic and
　cook for an additional 3 minutes, then add the
　tomatoes, breadcrumbs, and egg yolks and season to
　taste with salt and pepper. Cook, stirring occasionally
　and mashing the mixture with a wooden spoon, for an
　additional 10–15 minutes, or until thick and pulpy.

3 Meanwhile, scrub the clams under cold running water.
　Discard any with broken shells or any that do not close
　immediately when sharply tapped.

4 Place the clams in a large, heavy-bottom pan. Add
　the wine and bring to a boil. Cover and cook over high
　heat, shaking the pan occasionally, for 3–5 minutes,
　or until the clams have opened. Discard any that
　remain closed.

5 Using a slotted spoon, transfer the clams to warmed
　serving bowls. Strain the cooking liquid into the
　tomato sauce, then stir well and spoon over the clams.
　Sprinkle with the chopped egg whites and parsley
　and serve immediately, garnished with lemon wedges.

batter-fried fish sticks

ingredients

serves 6

generous ¾ cup all-purpose flour,
    plus extra for dusting
pinch of salt
1 egg, beaten
1 tbsp olive oil
⅔ cup water
1 lb 5 oz/600 g firm-fleshed
    whitefish fillet, such as
    monkfish or hake
sunflower or olive oil,
    for deep-frying
lemon wedges, for serving

method

1 To make the batter, put the flour and salt into a large
bowl and make a well in the center. Pour the egg
and olive oil into the well, then gradually add the
water, mixing in the flour from the side and beating
constantly, until all the flour is incorporated and a
smooth batter forms.

2 Cut the fish into sticks about ¾ inch/2 cm wide and
2 inches/5 cm long. Dust lightly with flour so that the
batter sticks to them when dipped in it.

3 Heat enough sunflower or olive oil for deep-frying in a
deep-fat fryer to 350–375°F/180–190°C, or until a cube
of bread browns in 30 seconds. Spear a fish stick onto
a toothpick and dip into the batter, then drop the fish
and toothpick into the hot oil. Cook the fish sticks,
in batches to avoid overcrowding, for 5 minutes, or
until golden brown. Remove with a slotted spoon
or draining basket and drain on paper towels. Keep hot
in a warm oven while cooking the remaining fish sticks.

4 Serve the fish sticks hot, with lemon wedges for
squeezing over.

monkfish, rosemary & bacon skewers

ingredients

makes 12

9 oz/250 g monkfish fillet
12 stalks of fresh rosemary
3 tbsp olive oil
juice of ½ small lemon
1 garlic clove, crushed
6 thick slices Canadian bacon
salt and pepper
lemon wedges, to garnish
dipping sauce, to serve

method

1 Slice the monkfish fillet in half lengthwise, then cut each fillet into 12 bite-size chunks to make a total of 24 pieces. Put the monkfish pieces in a large bowl.

2 To prepare the rosemary skewers, strip the leaves off the stalks and set them aside, leaving a few leaves at one end.

3 For the marinade, finely chop the reserved rosemary leaves and whisk together in a bowl with the olive oil, lemon juice, garlic, and salt and pepper. Add the monkfish pieces and toss until coated in the marinade. Cover and let marinate in the refrigerator for 1–2 hours.

4 Cut each bacon slice in half lengthwise, then in half widthwise, and roll up each piece. Thread two pieces of monkfish alternately with two bacon rolls onto the rosemary skewers.

5 Preheat the broiler and arrange the skewers so that the rosemary leaves do not catch fire. Broil the monkfish and bacon skewers for 10 minutes, turning from time to time and basting with the marinade until cooked. Serve hot, garnished with lemon wedges, and a bowl of dipping sauce.

traditional catalan salt cod salad

ingredients

serves 4–6

14 oz/400 g pre-soaked salt
    cod in 1 piece

6 scallions, thinly sliced on
    the diagonal

⅓ cup extra virgin olive oil

1 tbsp sherry vinegar

1 tbsp lemon juice

2 large red bell peppers, broiled,
    peeled, seeded, and
    very finely diced

12 large black olives, pitted
    and sliced

2 large, juicy tomatoes,
    thinly sliced

pepper

2 tbsp very finely chopped fresh
    parsley, to garnish

method

1 Pat the salt cod very dry with paper towels and remove
   the skin and bones, then use your fingers to tear into
   fine shreds. Place in a large, nonmetallic bowl with the
   scallions, olive oil, vinegar, and lemon juice and toss
   together. Season with pepper, then cover and let
   marinate in the refrigerator for 3 hours.

2 Stir in the bell peppers and olives. Taste and adjust the
   seasoning, if necessary, remembering that the cod and
   olives might be salty. Arrange the tomato slices on a
   large serving platter or individual serving plates and
   spoon the salad on top. Sprinkle with chopped parsley
   and serve.

catalan fish

ingredients

serves 4

4 globe artichokes, stems
cut off, tough outer
leaves removed and
discarded, and points of
the leaves trimmed with
kitchen scissors
2 soles, filleted
½ lemon
1 cup dry white wine
¼ cup butter
2 tbsp all-purpose flour
1 cup milk
freshly grated nutmeg
bay leaf
2 cups sliced mushrooms
salt and pepper

method

1 Place the artichokes in a pan and add water to cover
and a pinch of salt. Bring to a boil, then simmer for
30 minutes, or until tender.

2 Season the fish fillets to taste and squeeze over the
lemon. Cut each fillet into quarters lengthwise, roll up,
and secure with a toothpick. Place in a shallow pan,
then pour in the wine and poach gently, spooning
over the wine occasionally, for 15 minutes.

3 Melt half the butter in a pan, then add the flour and
cook, stirring constantly, for 2 minutes. Stir in the milk.
Bring to a boil, stirring constantly, until thickened and
smooth. Reduce the heat to very low, season to taste
with salt and pepper and nutmeg and add the bay leaf.

4 Melt the remaining butter in a skillet. Add the
mushrooms and cook over medium heat, stirring
occasionally, for 3 minutes. Remove from the heat.

5 Remove the artichokes from the pan with a slotted
spoon and drain on paper towels. Remove and
discard the hairy chokes and prickly leaves. Divide the
mushrooms between the artichoke cavities and spoon
in the sauce, discarding the bay leaf. Drain the fish
fillets with a slotted spoon and remove and discard
the toothpicks. Place two fillets in each of the artichoke
cavities and serve.

sardines with lemon & chile

ingredients

serves 4

1 lb/450 g fresh sardines, scaled,
    cleaned, and heads removed
¼ cup lemon juice
1 garlic clove, finely chopped
1 tbsp finely chopped fresh dill
1 tsp finely chopped
    fresh red chile
¼ cup olive oil
salt and pepper

method

1 Place the sardines, skin-side up, on a cutting board and press along the length of the spines with your thumbs. Turn them over and remove and discard the bones.

2 Place the fillets in a shallow, nonmetallic dish, skin-side down, and sprinkle with the lemon juice. Cover with plastic wrap and let stand in a refrigerator for 30 minutes.

3 Drain off any excess lemon juice. Sprinkle the garlic, dill, and chile over the fish and season to taste with salt and pepper. Drizzle over the olive oil, then cover with plastic wrap and let chill for 12 hours before serving.

sardines marinated in sherry vinegar

ingredients

serves 6

¾ cup olive oil

12 small fresh sardines, cleaned and filleted, and heads and tails removed if wished

⅓ cup sherry vinegar

2 carrots, cut into julienne strips

1 onion, thinly sliced

1 garlic clove, crushed

1 bay leaf

3 tbsp chopped fresh flat-leaf parsley

salt and pepper

few sprigs of fresh dill, to garnish

lemon wedges, to serve

method

1 Heat 4 tablespoons of the olive oil in a large, heavy-bottom skillet. Add the sardines and cook for 10 minutes, or until browned on both sides. Using a spatula, very carefully remove the sardines from the skillet and transfer to a large, shallow, nonmetallic dish that will hold the sardines in a single layer.

2 Gently heat the remaining olive oil and the sherry vinegar in a large pan, add the carrot strips, onion, garlic, and bay leaf and let simmer gently for 5 minutes, until softened. Season the vegetables to taste with salt and pepper. Let the mixture cool slightly, then pour the marinade over the sardines.

3 Cover the dish and let the sardines cool before transferring to the refrigerator. Let marinate for about 8 hours or overnight, spooning the marinade over the sardines occasionally. Return the sardines to room temperature before serving. Sprinkle with parsley, and garnish with dill sprigs. Serve with lemon wedges.

pickled mackerel

ingredients

serves 6

8 fresh mackerel fillets

1¼ cups extra virgin olive oil

2 large red onions, thinly sliced

2 carrots, sliced

2 bay leaves

2 garlic cloves, thinly sliced

2 dried red chiles

1 fennel bulb, halved and
thinly sliced

1¼ cups sherry vinegar

1½ tbsp coriander seeds

salt and pepper

toasted French bread slices,
to serve

method

1 Preheat the broiler. Place the mackerel fillets, skin-side up, on a broiler rack and brush with oil. Broil under a hot broiler, about 4 inches/10 cm from the heat source, for 4–6 minutes, until the skins become brown and crispy and the flesh flakes easily. Reserve until required.

2 Heat the remaining oil in a large skillet. Add the onions and cook for 5 minutes, until softened but not browned. Add the remaining ingredients and let simmer for 10 minutes, until the carrots are tender.

3 Flake the mackerel flesh into large pieces, removing the skin and tiny bones. Place the mackerel pieces in a preserving jar and pour over the onion, carrot, and fennel mixture. (The jar should accommodate everything packed in quite tightly with the minimum air gap at the top once the vegetable mixture has been poured in.) Let cool completely, then cover tightly and let chill for at least 24 hours and up to 5 days. Serve the pieces of mackerel on toasted slices of French bread with a little of the oil drizzled over.

4 Alternatively, serve the mackerel and its pickled vegetables as a first-course salad.

tuna, egg & potato salad

ingredients

serves 4

12 oz/350 g new potatoes, unpeeled
1 hard-cooked egg, cooled and shelled
3 tbsp olive oil
1½ tbsp white wine vinegar
4 oz/115 g canned tuna in oil, drained and flaked
2 shallots, finely chopped
1 tomato, peeled and diced
2 tbsp chopped fresh parsley
salt and pepper

method

1 Cook the potatoes in a pan of lightly salted boiling water for 10 minutes, then remove from the heat, cover, and let stand for 15–20 minutes, or until tender.

2 Meanwhile, slice the egg, then cut each slice in half. Whisk the olive oil and vinegar together in a bowl and season to taste with salt and pepper. Spoon a little of the vinaigrette into a serving dish to coat the base.

3 Drain the potatoes, then peel and thinly slice. Place half the slices over the base of the dish and season to taste with salt, then top with half the tuna, half the egg slices, and half the shallots. Pour over half the remaining dressing. Make a second layer with the remaining potato slices, tuna, egg, and shallots, then pour over the remaining dressing.

4 Finally, top the salad with the tomato and parsley. Cover with plastic wrap and let stand in a refrigerator for 1–2 hours before serving.

tuna rolls

ingredients

serves 4

3 red bell peppers
½ cup olive oil
2 tbsp lemon juice
scant ⅓ cup red wine vinegar
2 garlic cloves, finely chopped
1 tsp paprika
1 tsp dried chili flakes
2 tsp sugar
2 tbsp salted capers
7 oz/200 g canned tuna in oil,
    drained and flaked

method

1 Preheat the broiler. Place the bell peppers on a cookie sheet and cook under a hot broiler, turning frequently, for 10 minutes, until the skin is blackened and blistered all over. Using tongs, transfer the peppers to a plastic bag, then tie the top and let cool.

2 Meanwhile, whisk the olive oil, lemon juice, vinegar, garlic, paprika, chili flakes, and sugar together in a small bowl.

3 When the peppers are cool enough to handle, peel off the skins, core and seed then cut the flesh into thirds lengthwise. Place the pepper pieces in a nonmetallic dish and pour over the dressing, turning to coat. Let stand in a cool place for 30 minutes.

4 Rub the salt off the capers and mix with the tuna. Drain the pepper pieces, reserving the dressing. Divide the tuna mixture between the pepper pieces and roll up. Secure with wooden toothpicks. Place the tuna rolls on a serving platter, then spoon over the dressing and serve at room temperature.

anchovy & spinach empanadillas

ingredients

serves 6–8

1 lb 2 oz/500 g fresh
    spinach leaves
2 tbsp olive oil, plus extra
    for brushing
2 garlic cloves, finely chopped
8 canned anchovy fillets in oil,
    drained and chopped
2 tbsp raisins, soaked in hot
    water for 10 minutes
scant ⅓ cup pine nuts
1 lb/450 g puff pastry,
    thawed if frozen
all-purpose flour, for dusting
1 egg, lightly beaten
salt and pepper

method

1 Trim and discard any tough stems from the spinach and finely chop the leaves.

2 Heat the olive oil in a large pan. Add the chopped spinach, then cover and cook over low heat, gently shaking the pan occasionally, for 3 minutes. Stir in the garlic and anchovies and cook, uncovered, for an additional 1 minute. Remove the pan from the heat.

3 Drain the raisins and chop, then stir them into the spinach mixture with the pine nuts and salt and pepper to taste. Let cool.

4 Roll out the pastry on a lightly floured counter to a circle about ⅛ inch/3 mm thick. Stamp out circles using a 3-inch/7.5-cm cookie cutter. Re-roll the trimmings and stamp out more circles.

5 Place 1–2 heaped teaspoonfuls of the spinach filling onto each pastry round. Brush the edges with water and fold over to make half moons. Press together well to seal. Place the empanadillas on cookie sheets and brush with beaten egg to glaze, then bake in a preheated oven, 350°F/180°C, for 15 minutes, or until golden brown. Serve warm.

fried calamari

ingredients

serves 6

1 lb/450 g prepared squid
all-purpose flour, for coating
corn oil, for deep-frying
salt
lemon wedges, to garnish
aïoli sauce, to serve
(see page 36)

method

1 Make 1 quantity of aïoli sauce.

2 Slice the squid into ½-inch/1-cm rings and halve the tentacles if large. Rinse and dry well on paper towels so that they do not spit during cooking. Dust the squid rings with flour so that they are lightly coated. Do not season the flour, as this will toughen the squid.

3 Heat the oil in a deep-fryer to 350–375°F/180–190°C, or until a cube of bread browns in 30 seconds. Carefully add the squid rings, in batches so that the temperature of the oil does not drop, and deep-fry for 2–3 minutes, or until golden brown and crisp all over, turning several times. Do not overcook as the squid will become tough and rubbery rather than moist and tender.

4 Using a slotted spoon, remove the deep-fried squid from the deep-fryer and drain well on paper towels. Transfer to a warm oven while you deep-fry the remaining squid rings.

5 Sprinkle the deep-fried squid with salt and serve piping hot, garnished with lemon wedges for squeezing over them. Accompany with a bowl of aïoli to dip the pieces in.

giant garlic shrimp

ingredients

serves 4

½ cup olive oil
4 garlic cloves, finely chopped
2 hot fresh red chiles, seeded
    and finely chopped
1 lb/450 g cooked
    jumbo shrimp
2 tbsp chopped fresh
    flat-leaf parsley
salt and pepper
lemon wedges, to garnish
crusty bread, to serve

method

1 Heat the olive oil in a preheated wok or large,
   heavy-bottom skillet over low heat. Add the garlic and
   chiles and cook, stirring occasionally, for 1–2 minutes,
   until softened but not colored.

2 Add the shrimp and stir-fry for 2–3 minutes, or until
   heated through and coated in the garlic mixture.

3 Turn off the heat and add the chopped parsley, stirring
   well to mix. Season to taste with salt and pepper.

4 Divide the shrimp and garlic-flavored oil between
   warmed serving dishes and garnish with lemon
   wedges. Serve with crusty bread.

lime-drizzled shrimp

ingredients

serves 4

4 limes
12 raw jumbo shrimp,
    in their shells
3 tbsp olive oil
2 garlic cloves, finely chopped
splash of fino sherry
3 tbsp chopped fresh
    flat-leaf parsley
salt and pepper

method

1 Grate the rind and squeeze the juice from 2 of the limes. Cut the remaining 2 limes into wedges and set aside for later.

2 To prepare the shrimp, remove the head and legs, leaving the shells and tails intact. Using a sharp knife, make a shallow slit along the back of each shrimp, then pull out the dark vein and discard. Rinse the shrimp under cold water and dry on paper towels.

3 Heat the olive oil in a large, heavy-bottom skillet, then add the garlic and cook for 30 seconds. Add the shrimp and cook for 5 minutes, stirring from time to time, or until they turn pink and start to curl. Mix in the lime rind, juice, and a splash of sherry to moisten, then stir well together.

4 Transfer the cooked shrimp to a serving dish, season to taste with salt and pepper, and sprinkle with the parsley. Serve piping hot, accompanied by the reserved lime wedges for squeezing over the shrimp.

garlic shrimp with lemon & parsley

ingredients

serves 6

60 raw jumbo shrimp,
   thawed if using frozen
²/₃ cup olive oil
6 garlic cloves, thinly sliced
3 dried hot red chiles (optional)
¹/₃ cup freshly squeezed lemon juice
2¹/₄ oz/60 g very finely chopped
   fresh parsley
French bread, to serve

method

1 Peel and devein the shrimp and remove the heads, leaving the tails on. Rinse and pat the shrimp dry.

2 Heat the olive oil in a large, deep skillet. Add the garlic and chiles, if using, and stir constantly until they begin to sizzle. Add the shrimp and cook until they turn pink and begin to curl.

3 Use a slotted spoon to transfer the shrimp to warm earthenware bowls. Sprinkle each bowl with lemon juice and parsley. Serve with plenty of bread to mop up the juices.

baked scallops

ingredients

serves 4

1 lb 9 oz/700 g scallops,
    shucked and chopped
2 onions, finely chopped
2 garlic cloves, finely chopped
3 tbsp chopped fresh parsley
pinch of freshly grated nutmeg
pinch of ground cloves
2 tbsp fresh white breadcrumbs
2 tbsp olive oil
salt and pepper

method

1 Mix the scallops, onions, garlic, 2 tablespoons of the parsley, the nutmeg, and cloves together in a bowl and season to taste with salt and pepper.

2 Divide the mixture between 4 scrubbed scallop shells or heatproof dishes. Sprinkle the breadcrumbs and remaining parsley on top and drizzle with the olive oil.

3 Bake the scallops in a preheated oven, 400°F/200°C, for 15–20 minutes, or until lightly golden and piping hot. Serve immediately.

seared scallops

ingredients

serves 4–6

¼ cup olive oil
3 tbsp orange juice
2 tsp hazelnut oil
24 scallops, shucked
salad greens (optional)
6 oz/175 g cabrales or other
     blue cheese, crumbled
2 tbsp chopped fresh dill
salt and pepper

method

1 Whisk 3 tablespoons of the olive oil, the orange juice, and the hazelnut oil together in a pitcher and season to taste with salt and pepper.

2 Heat the remaining olive oil in a large, heavy-bottom skillet. Add the scallops and cook over high heat for 1 minute on each side, or until golden.

3 Transfer the scallops to a bed of salad greens or individual plates. Scatter over the cheese and dill, then drizzle with the dressing. Serve warm.

clams with fava beans

ingredients

serves 4–6

4 canned anchovy fillets
    in oil, drained

1 tsp salted capers

3 tbsp olive oil

1 tbsp sherry vinegar

1 tsp Dijon mustard

1 lb 2 oz/500 g fresh clams

about ¾ cup water

1 lb 2 oz/500 g fava beans,
    shelled if fresh

2 tbsp chopped mixed fresh herbs,
    such as parsley, chives,
    and mint

salt and pepper

method

1 Place the anchovies in a small bowl, then add water to cover and let soak for 5 minutes. Drain well, then pat dry with paper towels and place in a mortar. Brush the salt off the capers, then add to the mortar and pound to a paste with a pestle.

2 Whisk the olive oil, vinegar, and mustard together in a separate bowl, then whisk in the anchovy paste and season to taste with pepper. Cover with plastic wrap and let stand at room temperature until required.

3 Scrub the clams under cold running water. Discard any with broken shells or any that do not close immediately when sharply tapped. Place the clams in a large pan and add the water. Cover and bring to a boil over high heat. Cook, shaking the pan occasionally, for 3–5 minutes, or until the clams have opened. Discard any that remain closed.

4 Bring a large pan of lightly salted water to a boil. Add the fava beans, then return to a boil and blanch for 5 minutes. Drain, then refresh under cold running water and drain well again. Remove and discard the outer skins and place the fava beans in a bowl.

5 Drain the clams and remove them from their shells. Add to the beans and sprinkle with the herbs. Add the anchovy vinaigrette and toss lightly. Serve warm.

# of eggs
& cheese

asparagus scrambled eggs

ingredients

serves 6

1 lb/450 g asparagus, trimmed
    and coarsely chopped
2 tbsp olive oil
1 onion, finely chopped
1 garlic clove, finely chopped
6 eggs
1 tbsp water
6 small slices country bread
salt and pepper

method

1 Steam the asparagus pieces for 8 minutes or cook in
a large pan of lightly salted boiling water for 4 minutes,
or until just tender, depending on their thickness. Drain
well, if necessary.

2 Meanwhile, heat the oil in a large skillet, then add
the onion and cook over medium heat, stirring
occasionally, for 5 minutes, or until softened but not
browned. Add the garlic and cook, stirring, for
30 seconds until softened.

3 Stir the asparagus into the skillet and cook, stirring
occasionally, for 3–4 minutes. Meanwhile, break
the eggs into a bowl, then add the water and beat
together. Season to taste with salt and pepper.

4 Add the beaten eggs to the asparagus mixture and
cook, stirring constantly, for 2 minutes, or until the
eggs have just set. Remove from the heat.

5 Preheat the broiler. Toast the bread slices until golden
brown on both sides. Pile the scrambled eggs on top
of the toast and serve immediately.

stuffed eggs with anchovies & cheese

ingredients

serves 8

8 eggs

1¾ oz/50 g canned anchovy fillets in olive oil, drained

generous ½ cup grated Manchego cheese

¼ cup extra virgin olive oil

1 tbsp freshly squeezed lemon juice

1 garlic clove, crushed

4 pitted black Spanish olives, halved

4 pitted green Spanish olives, halved

hot or sweet smoked Spanish paprika, for dusting

salt and pepper

method

1 Put the eggs in a pan, then cover with cold water and slowly bring to a boil. Reduce the heat and simmer gently for 10 minutes. Immediately drain the eggs and rinse under cold running water to cool. Gently tap the eggs to crack the shells and let stand until cold.

2 When the eggs are cold, crack the shells all over and remove them. Using a stainless steel knife, halve the eggs, then carefully remove the egg yolks and put the yolks in a food processor.

3 Add the anchovy fillets, Manchego cheese, oil, lemon juice, and garlic to the egg yolks and process to a purée. Season to taste with salt and pepper.

4 Using a teaspoon, spoon the mixture into the egg white halves. Alternatively, using a pastry bag fitted with a ½-inch/1-cm plain tip, pipe the mixture into the egg white halves. Arrange the stuffed eggs on a serving dish, then cover and let chill in the refrigerator until ready to serve.

5 To serve, put an olive half on the top of each stuffed egg and dust with paprika.

chorizo & fava bean tortilla

ingredients

serves 9

8 oz/225 g frozen baby
    fava beans
6 eggs
3½ oz/100 g chorizo sausage,
    outer casing removed,
    chopped
3 tbsp olive oil
1 onion, chopped
salt and pepper

method

1 Cook the fava beans in a pan of boiling water for
   4 minutes. Drain well and let cool. Meanwhile, lightly
   beat the eggs in a large bowl. Add the chorizo sausage
   and season to taste with salt and pepper.

2 When the beans are cool enough to handle, slip off
   their skins. This is a laborious task, but worth doing
   if you have the time. This quantity will take about
   15 minutes to skin.

3 Heat the oil in a large skillet, then add the onion and
   cook over medium heat, stirring occasionally, for
   5 minutes, or until softened but not browned. Add
   the fava beans and cook, stirring, for 1 minute. Pour
   the egg mixture into the skillet and cook gently for
   2–3 minutes, or until the underside is just set and
   lightly browned. Use a spatula to loosen the tortilla
   away from the side and bottom of the skillet to let the
   uncooked egg run underneath and prevent the tortilla
   from sticking to the bottom.

4 Cover the tortilla with a large, upside-down plate and
   invert the tortilla onto it. Slide the tortilla back into
   the skillet, cooked-side up, and cook for an additional
   2–3 minutes, or until the underside is lightly browned.

5 Slide the tortilla onto a warmed serving dish. Serve
   warm, cut into small cubes.

spinach & mushroom tortilla

ingredients

serves 8

2 tbsp olive oil

3 shallots, finely chopped

12 oz/350 g sliced mushrooms

10 oz/280 g fresh spinach leaves, coarse stems removed

½ cup toasted slivered almonds

5 eggs

2 tbsp chopped fresh parsley

2 tbsp cold water

scant 1 cup grated mature Mahon, Manchego, or Parmesan cheese

salt and pepper

method

1 Heat the olive oil in a skillet that can safely be placed under the broiler. Add the shallots and cook over low heat, stirring occasionally, for 5 minutes, or until softened. Add the mushrooms and cook, stirring frequently, for an additional 4 minutes. Add the spinach, then increase the heat to medium and cook, stirring frequently, for 3–4 minutes, or until wilted. Reduce the heat, then season to taste with salt and pepper and stir in the slivered almonds.

2 Beat the eggs with the parsley, water, and salt and pepper to taste in a bowl. Pour the mixture into the skillet and cook for 5–8 minutes, or until the underside is set. Lift the edge of the tortilla occasionally to let the uncooked egg run underneath.

3 Preheat the broiler. Sprinkle the grated cheese over the tortilla and cook under a hot broiler for 3 minutes, or until the top is set and the cheese has melted. Serve, lukewarm or cold, cut into thin wedges.

tortilla española

ingredients

serves 4

1½ cups olive oil
1 lb/450 g waxy potatoes
2 onions, chopped
4 large eggs
salt and pepper
sprigs of fresh flat-leaf parsley,
    to garnish
olives, to serve (optional)

method

1 Heat the olive oil in a large, heavy-bottom skillet. Add the potato cubes and onions, then lower the heat and cook, stirring frequently, for 20 minutes, or until tender but not browned. Drain the potatoes and onions well. Set aside the oil.

2 Beat the eggs lightly in a large bowl and season well with salt and pepper. Stir in the potatoes and onions.

3 Wipe out the skillet with paper towels and heat 2 tablespoons of the reserved olive oil. When hot, add the egg and potato mixture, lower the heat and cook for 3–5 minutes, or until the underside is just set. Use a spatula to submerge the potatoes down into the egg and loosen the tortilla from the bottom of the skillet to stop it sticking.

4 Cover the tortilla with a plate, and hold the plate in place with the other hand. Drain off the oil in the skillet, then quickly invert the tortilla onto the plate. Return the skillet to the heat and add a little more oil if necessary. Slide the tortilla, cooked side uppermost, back into the skillet and cook for an additional 3–5 minutes, or until set underneath.

5 Slide the tortilla onto a serving plate and let stand for about 15 minutes. Serve warm or cold in slices, with olives if wished, garnished with parsley sprigs.

spicy stuffed eggs

ingredients

serves 6

6 hard-cooked eggs, cooled
    and shelled
scant 1 cup grated Manchego
    or cheddar cheese
1–2 tbsp mayonnaise
2 tbsp snipped fresh chives
1 fresh red chile, seeded and
    finely chopped
salt and pepper
salad greens, to serve

method

1 Cut the eggs in half lengthwise and, using a teaspoon, carefully scoop out the yolks into a fine strainer, reserving the egg white halves. Rub the yolks through the strainer into a bowl and add the grated cheese, mayonnaise, chives, chile, and salt and pepper to taste. Spoon the filling into the egg white halves.

2 Arrange a bed of salad greens on individual serving plates and top with the eggs. Cover and let chill in the refrigerator until ready to serve.

flamenco eggs

ingredients

serves 4

¼ cup olive oil
1 onion, thinly sliced
2 garlic cloves, finely chopped
2 small red bell peppers, seeded
    and chopped
4 tomatoes, peeled, seeded,
    and chopped
1 tbsp chopped fresh parsley
7 oz/200 g canned corn kernels,
    drained
4 eggs
salt and cayenne pepper

method

1 Heat the olive oil in a large, heavy-bottom skillet. Add the onion and garlic and cook over low heat, stirring occasionally, for 5 minutes, or until softened. Add the red bell peppers and cook, stirring occasionally, for an additional 10 minutes. Stir in the tomatoes and parsley, season to taste with salt and cayenne pepper and cook for an additional 5 minutes. Stir in the corn kernels and remove the skillet from the heat.

2 Divide the mixture among four individual ovenproof dishes. Make a hollow in the surface of each using the back of a spoon. Break an egg into each hollow.

3 Bake in a preheated oven, 350°F/180°C, for 15–25 minutes, or until the eggs have set. Serve hot.

basque scrambled eggs

ingredients

serves 4–6

¼ cup olive oil

1 large onion, finely chopped

1 large red bell pepper, seeded and chopped

1 large green bell pepper, seeded and chopped

2 large tomatoes, peeled, seeded, and chopped

2 oz/55 g chorizo sausage, thinly sliced, outer casing removed, if preferred

2½ tbsp butter

10 large eggs, lightly beaten

salt and pepper

4–6 thick slices country-style bread, toasted, to serve

method

1 Heat 2 tablespoons of olive oil in a large, heavy-bottom skillet over medium heat. Add the onion and bell peppers and cook for 5 minutes, or until the vegetables are softened but not browned. Add the tomatoes and heat through. Transfer to a heatproof plate and keep warm in a preheated low oven.

2 Add another tablespoon of oil to the skillet. Add the chorizo and cook for 30 seconds, just to warm through and flavor the oil. Add the sliced chorizo to the reserved vegetables.

3 Add a little extra olive oil, if necessary, to the skillet to bring it back to 2 tablespoons. Add the butter and let melt. Season the eggs with salt and pepper, then add to the pan and scramble until cooked to the desired degree of firmness. Return the vegetables and chorizo to the pan and stir through. Serve immediately on hot toast.

chorizo & quail's eggs

ingredients

serves 12

12 slices French bread,
    sliced on the diagonal,
    about $\frac{1}{4}$ inch/5 mm thick
1$\frac{1}{2}$ oz/40 g cured, ready-to-eat
    chorizo, cut into 12 thin slices
olive oil
12 quail's eggs
mild paprika
salt and pepper
fresh flat-leaf parsley,
    to garnish

method

1 Preheat the broiler to high. Arrange the slices of bread on a cookie sheet and broil until golden on both sides.

2 Cut or fold the thin chorizo slices to fit on the toasts, then reserve.

3 Heat a thin layer of olive oil in a large skillet over medium heat. Break the eggs into the skillet and cook, spooning the fat over the yolks, until the whites are set and the yolks are cooked to your liking.

4 Remove the fried eggs from the skillet and drain on paper towels. Immediately transfer to the chorizo-topped toasts and dust with paprika. Season to taste with salt and pepper, then garnish with parsley and serve immediately.

deep-fried manchego cheese

ingredients

serves 6–8

7 oz/200 g Manchego cheese
3 tbsp all-purpose flour
1 egg
1 tsp water
1½ cups fresh white or brown
    breadcrumbs
corn oil, for deep-frying
salt and pepper

method

1 Slice the cheese into triangular shapes about ¾ inch/
2 cm thick. Put the flour in a plastic bag and season
with salt and pepper to taste. Break the egg into a
shallow dish and beat together with the water. Spread
out the breadcrumbs on a plate.

2 Toss the cheese pieces in the flour so that they are
evenly coated, then dip the cheese in the egg mixture.
Finally, dip the cheese in the breadcrumbs so that the
pieces are coated on all sides.

3 Just before serving, heat about 1 inch/2.5 cm of the
corn oil in a large, heavy-bottom skillet or heat the
oil in a deep-fryer to 350–375°F/180–190°C, or until a
cube of bread browns in 30 seconds. Add the cheese
pieces, in batches of about four or five pieces so that
the temperature of the oil does not drop, and deep-fry
for 1–2 minutes, turning once, until the cheese is just
starting to melt and they are golden brown on all sides.
Do make sure that the oil is hot enough, otherwise the
coating on the cheese will take too long to become
crisp and the cheese inside may ooze out.

4 Using a slotted spoon, remove the cheese from the
skillet or deep-fryer and drain well on paper towels.
Serve hot.

cheese puffs with fiery tomato salsa

ingredients

serves 8

scant ½ cup all-purpose flour
¼ cup olive oil
⅔ cup water
2 eggs, beaten
½ cup finely grated Manchego,
    Parmesan, cheddar, Gouda,
    or Gruyère cheese
½ tsp paprika
corn oil, for deep-frying
salt and pepper

tomato salsa

2 tbsp olive oil
1 small onion, finely chopped
1 garlic clove, crushed
splash of dry white wine
14 oz/400 g canned chopped
    tomatoes
1 tbsp tomato paste
¼–½ tsp dried red pepper flakes
dash of Tabasco sauce
pinch of sugar
salt and pepper

method

1 To make the salsa, heat the olive oil in a pan, add the onion, and cook until softened but not browned. Add the garlic and cook for 30 seconds. Add the wine and let bubble, then add the remaining salsa ingredients and let simmer, uncovered, until a thick sauce is formed. Set aside until ready to serve.

2 Meanwhile, prepare the cheese puffs. Sift the flour onto a plate. Put the olive oil and water in a pan and slowly bring to a boil. As soon as the water boils, remove the pan from the heat, and quickly tip in the flour. Using a wooden spoon, beat the mixture well until it is smooth and leaves the sides of the pan.

3 Let cool for 1–2 minutes, then gradually add the eggs, beating hard after each addition and keeping the mixture stiff. Add the cheese and paprika, season to taste with salt and pepper, and mix well together.

4 To cook the cheese puffs, heat the corn oil in a deep-fryer to 350–375°F/180–190°C. Drop teaspoonfuls of the prepared mixture, in batches, into the hot oil and deep-fry for 2–3 minutes, turning once, or until golden and crispy. They should rise to the surface and puff up. Drain well. Serve the puffs piping hot, with the salsa.

figs with blue cheese

ingredients

serves 6

12 ripe figs
3 cups Spanish blue cheese,
    crumbled
extra virgin olive oil, to serve

caramelized almonds

½ cup superfine sugar
scant 1 cup whole almonds
butter, for greasing

method

1 First make the caramelized almonds. Place the sugar in a pan over medium heat and stir until the sugar melts and turns golden brown and bubbles. Do not stir once the mixture begins to bubble. Remove the pan from the heat, then add the almonds one at a time and quickly turn with a fork until coated. If the caramel hardens, return the pan to the heat. Transfer each almond to a lightly greased cookie sheet once it is coated. Let stand until cool and firm.

2 To serve, slice the figs in half and arrange four halves on individual serving plates. Coarsely chop the almonds by hand. Place a mound of blue cheese on each plate and sprinkle with chopped almonds. Drizzle the figs very lightly with the olive oil.

cheese & shallots with herb dressing

ingredients

serves 6

1 tsp sesame seeds
1/4 tsp cumin seeds
4 tomatoes, seeded and diced
scant 1/3 cup olive oil
1/4 cup lemon juice
2 tsp chopped fresh thyme
1 tbsp chopped fresh mint
4 shallots, finely chopped
1 lb 2 oz/500 g Idiazabal or other
    sheep's milk cheese, diced
salt and pepper

method

1 Dry-fry the sesame and cumin seeds in a small, heavy-bottom skillet, shaking the skillet frequently, until they begin to pop and give off their aroma. Remove the skillet from the heat and let cool.

2 Place the tomatoes in a bowl. To make the dressing, whisk the olive oil and lemon juice together in a separate bowl. Season to taste with salt and pepper, then add the thyme, mint, and shallots and mix well.

3 Place the cheese in another bowl. Pour half the dressing over the tomatoes and toss lightly. Cover with plastic wrap and let chill in the refrigerator for 1 hour. Pour the remaining dressing over the cheese, then also cover and chill in the refrigerator for 1 hour.

4 To serve, divide the cheese mixture among six serving plates and sprinkle with half the toasted seeds. Top with the tomato mixture and sprinkle with the remaining toasted seeds.

roasted bell peppers with fiery cheese

ingredients

serves 6

1 red bell pepper, halved
   and seeded
1 orange bell pepper, halved
   and seeded
1 yellow bell pepper, halved
   and seeded
4 oz/115 g Afuega'l Pitu cheese
   or other hot spiced
   cheese, diced
1 tbsp clear honey
1 tbsp sherry vinegar
salt and pepper

method

1 Preheat the broiler. Place the peppers, skin-side up, in a single layer on a cookie sheet. Cook under the broiler for 8–10 minutes or until the skins have blistered and blackened. Using tongs, transfer to a plastic bag. Tie the top and set aside to cool.

2 When the peppers are cool enough to handle, peel off the skin with your fingers or a knife and discard it. Place on a serving plate and sprinkle over the cheese.

3 Whisk the honey and vinegar together in a bowl and season to taste with salt and pepper. Pour the dressing over the peppers, then cover and chill in the refrigerator until required.

burgos with sherry vinegar

ingredients

serves 4

14 oz/400 g Burgos cheese
1–2 tbsp clear honey
3 tbsp sherry vinegar
carrot sticks
chilled sherry, to serve

method

1 Place the cheese in a bowl and beat until smooth, then beat in 1 tablespoon of the honey and 1½ tablespoons of the vinegar.

2 Taste and adjust the sweetness to taste by adding more honey or more vinegar as required.

3 Divide among four small serving bowls, then cover and let chill in the refrigerator until required. Serve with carrot sticks and chilled sherry.

cheese & olive empanadillas

ingredients

makes 26

3 oz/85 g firm or soft cheese
½ cup pitted green olives
¼ cup sundried tomatoes in oil,
    drained
1¾ oz/50 g canned anchovies,
    drained
2 tbsp sundried tomato paste
all-purpose flour, for dusting
1 lb 2 oz/500 g ready-made
    puff pastry, thawed if frozen
beaten egg, to glaze
fresh flat-leaf parsley sprigs,
    to garnish
pepper

method

1 Cut the cheese into small dice measuring about
   ¼ inch/5 mm. Chop the olives, sundried tomatoes,
   and anchovies into pieces about the same size as the
   cheese. Put all the chopped ingredients in a bowl,
   season with pepper to taste, and gently mix together.
   Stir in the sundried tomato paste.

2 On a lightly floured counter, thinly roll out the puff
   pastry. Using a plain, round 3¼-inch/8-cm cutter, cut
   into 18 circles. Gently pile the trimmings together, roll
   out again, then cut out an additional 8 circles. Using a
   teaspoon, put a little of the prepared filling equally in
   the center of each circle.

3 Dampen the edges of the pastry with a little water,
   then bring up the sides to completely cover the filling
   and pinch the edges together with your fingers to seal
   them. With the tip of a sharp knife, make a small slit in
   the top of each pastry. You can store the pastries in the
   refrigerator until you are ready to bake them.

4 Place the pastries onto dampened cookie sheets and
   brush each with a little beaten egg to glaze. Bake in
   a preheated oven, 400°F/200°C, for 10–15 minutes,
   or until golden brown, crisp and well risen. Serve the
   empanadillas piping hot, warm, or cold, garnished
   with parsley sprigs.

index